*Presented to:*

_____

*By:*

_____

# GOD'S
# PROMISES®

— & —

# ANSWERS

FOR WOMEN

COUNTRYMAN®

A Division of Thomas Nelson
Nashville

Cover design by David Uttley, David Uttley Design, Sisters, Oregon.

ISBN: 1-4041-0031-8

Printed in Mexico

# CONTENTS

## GOD'S PROMISES FOR WOMEN

*Contents*

## Contents

# *Contents*

## Contents

## GOD'S ANSWERS FOR WOMEN

### BEGINNING IN CHRIST

### GROWING IN CHRIST

*Contents*

MATURING IN CHRIST

## Contents

*God's Promises*

God's Plan For
Women is to . . .

Give unto the LORD, O you mighty ones,
Give unto the LORD glory and strength.
Give unto the LORD the glory due to
    His name;
Worship the LORD in the beauty of holiness.

PSALM 29:1–2

Oh come, let us worship and bow down;
Let us kneel before the LORD our Maker.
For He is our God,
And we are the people of His pasture,
And the sheep of His hand.
Today, if you will hear His voice.

PSALM 95:6–7

The hour is coming, and now is, when the true worshipers will worship the Father in spirit and truth; for the Father is seeking such to worship Him. God is Spirit, and those who worship Him must worship in spirit and truth.

JOHN 4:23–24

Oh, worship the LORD in the beauty of
    holiness!
Tremble before Him, all the earth.

PSALM 96:9

Then you will call upon Me and go and pray to Me,
and I will listen to you. And you will seek Me and
find Me, when you search for Me with all your heart.

JEREMIAH 29:12–13

Seek the LORD and His strength;
Seek His face evermore!
Remember His marvelous works which
    He has done,
His wonders, and the judgments of
    His mouth.

1 CHRONICLES 16:11–12

Blessed are those who keep His testimonies,
Who seek Him with the whole heart!
With my whole heart I have sought You;
Oh, let me not wander from Your
    commandments!

PSALM 119:2, 10

Thus I will bless You while I live;
I will lift up my hands in Your name.
My soul shall be satisfied as with marrow
    and fatness,
And my mouth shall praise You with
    joyful lips.

PSALM 63:4–5

# GOD'S PLAN FOR WOMEN IS TO . . . OBEY HIM

But be doers of the word, and not hearers only, deceiving yourselves.

JAMES 1:22

If you love Me, keep My commandments.

JOHN 14:15

Peter and the other apostles answered and said: "We ought to obey God rather than men."

ACTS 5:29

Whoever comes to Me, and hears My sayings and does them, I will show you whom he is like: He is like a man building a house, who dug deep and laid the foundation on the rock. And when the flood arose, the stream beat vehemently against that house, and could not shake it, for it was founded on the rock. But he who heard and did nothing is like a man who built a house on the earth without a foundation, against which the stream beat vehemently; and immediately it fell. And the ruin of that house was great.

LUKE 6:47–49

He who is faithful in what is least is faithful also in much; and he who is unjust in what is least is unjust also in much.

LUKE 16:10

We have had human fathers who corrected us, and we paid them respect. Shall we not much more readily be in subjection to the Father of spirits and live? For they indeed for a few days chastened us as seemed best to them, but He for our profit, that we may be partakers of His holiness.

HEBREWS 12:9–10

The world is passing away, and the lust of it; but he who does the will of God abides forever.

1 JOHN 2:17

Now the just shall live by faith;
But if anyone draws back,
My soul has no pleasure in him.

HEBREWS 10:38

Let us therefore come boldly to the throne of grace, that we may obtain mercy and find grace to help in time of need.

HEBREWS 4:16

Evening and morning and at noon
I will pray, and cry aloud,
And He shall hear my voice.

PSALM 55:17

Give ear, O LORD, to my prayer;
And attend to the voice of my supplications.
In the day of my trouble I will call upon You,
For You will answer me.

PSALM 86:6–7

For the eyes of the LORD are on the
righteous,
And His ears are open to their prayers;
But the face of the LORD is against those
who do evil.

1 PETER 3:12

Then He spoke a parable to them, that men always ought to pray and not lose heart.

LUKE 18:1

When you pray, you shall not be like the hypocrites. For they love to pray standing in the synagogues and on the corners of the streets, that they may be seen by men. Assuredly, I say to you, they have their reward. But you, when you pray, go into your room, and when you have shut your door, pray to your Father who is in the secret place; and your Father who sees in secret will reward you openly.

MATTHEW 6:5–6

> You will make your prayer to Him,
> He will hear you,
> And you will pay your vows.
> You will also declare a thing,
> And it will be established for you;
> So light will shine on your ways.

JOB 22:27–28

Let him ask in faith, with no doubting, for he who doubts is like a wave of the sea driven and tossed by the wind.

JAMES 1:6

# GOD'S PLAN FOR WOMEN IS TO . . . LISTEN TO THE HOLY SPIRIT

For what man knows the things of a man except the spirit of the man which is in him? Even so no one knows the things of God except the Spirit of God. Now we have received, not the spirit of the world, but the Spirit who is from God, that we might know the things that have been freely given to us by God.

These things we also speak, not in words which man's wisdom teaches but which the Holy Spirit teaches, comparing spiritual things with spiritual.

1 CORINTHIANS 2:11–13

For the Holy Spirit will teach you in that very hour what you ought to say.

LUKE 12:12

Speaking the truth in love, may grow up in all things into Him who is the head—Christ— from whom the whole body, joined and knit together by what every joint supplies, according to the effective working by which every part does its share, causes growth of the body for the edifying of itself in love.

Do not grieve the Holy Spirit of God, by whom you were sealed for the day of redemption.

EPHESIANS 4:15–16, 30

9

You, beloved, building yourselves up on your most holy faith, praying in the Holy Spirit, keep yourselves in the love of God, looking for the mercy of our Lord Jesus Christ unto eternal life.

JUDE 20–21

Nevertheless I tell you the truth. It is to your advantage that I go away; for if I do not go away, the Helper will not come to you; but if I depart, I will send Him to you. And when He has come, He will convict the world of sin, and of righteousness, and of judgment: of sin, because they do not believe in Me; of righteousness, because I go to My Father and you see Me no more; of judgment, because the ruler of this world is judged.

I still have many things to say to you, but you cannot bear them now.

JOHN 16:7–12

Knowing this first, that no prophecy of Scripture is of any private interpretation, for prophecy never came by the will of man, but holy men of God spoke as they were moved by the Holy Spirit.

2 PETER 1:20–21

If the Spirit of Him who raised Jesus from the dead dwells in you, He who raised Christ from the dead will also give life to your mortal bodies through His Spirit who dwells in you.

The Spirit Himself bears witness with our spirit that we are children of God, and if children, then heirs—heirs of God and joint heirs with Christ, if indeed we suffer with Him, that we may also be glorified together.

For I consider that the sufferings of this present time are not worthy to be compared with the glory which shall be revealed in us.

Likewise the Spirit also helps in our weaknesses. For we do not know what we should pray for as we ought, but the Spirit Himself makes intercession for us with groanings which cannot be uttered. Now He who searches the hearts knows what the mind of the Spirit is, because He makes intercession for the saints according to the will of God.

ROMANS 8:11, 16–18, 26–27

But the Helper, the Holy Spirit, whom the Father will send in My name, He will teach you all things, and bring to your remembrance all things that I said to you.

JOHN 14:26

Being assembled together with them, He commanded them not to depart from Jerusalem, but to wait for the Promise of the Father, "which," He said, "you have heard from Me; for John truly baptized with water, but you shall be baptized with the Holy Spirit not many days from now."

And He said to them, "It is not for you to know times or seasons which the Father has put in His own authority. But you shall receive power when the Holy Spirit has come upon you; and you shall be witnesses to Me in Jerusalem, and in all Judea and Samaria, and to the end of the earth."

ACTS 1:4–5, 7–8

Not that we are sufficient of ourselves to think of anything as being from ourselves, but our sufficiency is from God, who also made us sufficient as ministers of the new covenant, not of the letter but of the Spirit; for the letter kills, but the Spirit gives life.

Now the Lord is the Spirit; and where the Spirit of the Lord is, there is liberty. But we all, with unveiled face, beholding as in a mirror the glory of the Lord, are being transformed into the same image from glory to glory, just as by the Spirit of the Lord.

2 CORINTHIANS 3:5–6, 17–18

GOD TEACHES
WOMEN TO WALK IN
HIS WORD BY . . .

Praise the LORD!
Sing to the LORD a new song,
And His praise in the assembly of saints.

PSALM 149:1

Praise the LORD!
Oh, give thanks to the LORD, for He is good!
For His mercy endures forever.
Who can utter the mighty acts of the LORD?
Who can declare all His praise?

PSALM 106:1–2

Praise the LORD!
Praise, O servants of the LORD,
Praise the name of the LORD!
Blessed be the name of the LORD
From this time forth and forevermore!
From the rising of the sun to its going down
The LORD's name is to be praised.

PSALM 113:1–3

I will praise the name of God with a song,
And will magnify Him with thanksgiving.

PSALM 69:30

14

*God's Promises*

My heart is steadfast, O God, my heart
    is steadfast;
I will sing and give praise.
Awake, my glory!
Awake, lute and harp!
I will awaken the dawn.
I will praise You, O Lord, among the peoples;
I will sing to You among the nations.

PSALM 57:7–9

Praise the LORD!
Praise the LORD, O my soul!
While I live I will praise the LORD;
I will sing praises to my God while I have
    my being.

PSALM 146:1–2

Great is the LORD, and greatly to be praised
In the city of our God,
In His holy mountain.

PSALM 48:1

Every good gift and every perfect gift is from above,
and comes down from the Father of lights.

JAMES 1:17

*God's Promises*

Because Your lovingkindness is better
    than life,
My lips shall praise You.
Thus I will bless You while I live;
I will lift up my hands in Your name.
My soul shall be satisfied as with marrow
    and fatness,
And my mouth shall praise You with
    joyful lips.

PSALM 63:3–5

It shall come to pass
That before they call, I will answer;
And while they are still speaking, I will hear.

ISAIAH 65:24

You will keep him in perfect peace,
Whose mind is stayed on You,
Because he trusts in You.
Trust in the LORD forever,
For in YAH, the LORD, is everlasting strength.

ISAIAH 26:3–4

Behold, God is my salvation,
I will trust and not be afraid;
For YAH, the LORD, is my strength and song;
He also has become my salvation.

ISAIAH 12:2

The LORD is on my side;
I will not fear.
What can man do to me?
It is better to trust in the LORD
Than to put confidence in man.

PSALM 118:6, 8

In You, O LORD, I put my trust;
Let me never be put to shame.
For You are my hope, O Lord GOD;
You are my trust from my youth.
Let my mouth be filled with Your praise
And with Your glory all the day.

PSALM 71:1, 5, 8

Yes, we had the sentence of death in ourselves, that we should not trust in ourselves but in God who raises the dead, who delivered us from so great a death, and does deliver us; in whom we trust that He will still deliver us.

2 CORINTHIANS 1:9–10

He will not be afraid of evil tidings;
His heart is steadfast, trusting in the LORD.
His heart is established;
He will not be afraid,
Until he sees his desire upon his enemies.

PSALM 112:7–8

The salvation of the righteous is from
      the LORD;
He is their strength in the time of trouble.
And the LORD shall help them and
      deliver them;
He shall deliver them from the wicked,
And save them,
Because they trust in Him.

PSALM 37:39–40

For thus says the Lord GOD, the Holy
  One of Israel:
"In returning and rest you shall be saved;
In quietness and confidence shall be
  your strength."

ISAIAH 30:15

His work is honorable and glorious,
And His righteousness endures forever.
He has made His wonderful works to
  be remembered;
The LORD is gracious and full of
  compassion.

PSALM 111:3–4

We are always confident, knowing that while
we are at home in the body we are absent from the
Lord. For we walk by faith, not by sight.

2 CORINTHIANS 5:6–7

Fear not, for I am with you;
Be not dismayed, for I am your God.
I will strengthen you,
Yes, I will help you,
I will uphold you with My righteous right hand.

ISAIAH 41:10


God is our refuge and strength,
A very present help in trouble.
Therefore we will not fear,
Even though the earth be removed,
And though the mountains be carried
    into the midst of the sea;
Though its waters roar and be troubled,
Though the mountains shake with
    its swelling.

PSALM 46:1–3


Hungry and thirsty,
Their soul fainted in them.
Then they cried out to the LORD in
    their trouble,
And He delivered them out of their distresses.
And He led them forth by the right way,
That they might go to a city for a
    dwelling place.

PSALM 107:5–7

God has not given us a spirit of fear, but of power and of love and of a sound mind.

Who has saved us and called us with a holy calling, not according to our works, but according to His own purpose and grace which was given to us in Christ Jesus before time began.

2 TIMOTHY 1:7, 9

Come to Me, all you who labor and are heavy laden, and I will give you rest. Take My yoke upon you and learn from Me, for I am gentle and lowly in heart, and you will find rest for your souls. For My yoke is easy and My burden is light.

MATTHEW 11:28–30

For He Himself has said, "I will never leave you nor forsake you."

HEBREWS 13:5

I am the God of your father Abraham; do not fear, for I am with you.

GENESIS 26:24

Evening and morning and at noon
I will pray, and cry aloud,
And He shall hear my voice.

PSALM 55:17

Now when Daniel knew that the writing was signed, he went home. And in his upper room, with his windows open toward Jerusalem, he knelt down on his knees three times that day, and prayed and gave thanks before his God, as was his custom since early days.

DANIEL 6:10

Seven times a day I praise You,
Because of Your righteous judgments.

PSALM 119:164

I will meditate on Your precepts,
And contemplate Your ways.
I will delight myself in Your statutes;
I will not forget Your word.

PSALM 119:15–16

Your word is a lamp to my feet
And a light to my path.

PSALM 119:105

So then faith comes by hearing, and hearing by the word of God.

ROMANS 10:17

These are the ones sown on good ground, those who hear the word, accept it, and bear fruit: some thirty-fold, some sixty, and some a hundred.

MARK 4:20

The LORD is far from the wicked,
But He hears the prayer of the righteous.

PROVERBS 15:29

Pray without ceasing.

1 THESSALONIANS 5:17

For the commandment is a lamp,
And the law a light;
Reproofs of instruction are the way of life.

PROVERBS 6:23

Be diligent to present yourself approved to God, a worker who does not need to be ashamed, rightly dividing the word of truth.

2 TIMOTHY 2:15

Your word I have hidden in my heart,
That I might not sin against You.
Blessed are You, O LORD!
Teach me Your statutes!

PSALM 119:11–12

For in Him we live and move and have our being, as also some of your own poets have said, "For we are also His offspring."

ACTS 17:28

Whoever transgresses and does not abide in the doctrine of Christ does not have God. He who abides in the doctrine of Christ has both the Father and the Son.

2 JOHN 1:9

Draw near to God and He will draw near to you. Cleanse your hands, you sinners; and purify your hearts, you double-minded.

JAMES 4:8

Jesus said to him, "If you can believe, all things are possible to him who believes."

MARK 9:23

Those who are Christ's have crucified the flesh with its passions and desires. If we live in the Spirit, let us also walk in the Spirit.

GALATIANS 5:24–25

How sweet are Your words to my taste,
Sweeter than honey to my mouth!

PSALM 119:103

The law of the LORD is perfect,
         converting the soul;
The testimony of the LORD is sure,
         making wise the simple;
The statutes of the LORD are right,
         rejoicing the heart;
The commandment of the LORD is pure,
         enlightening the eyes;
More to be desired are they than gold,
Yea, than much fine gold;
Sweeter also than honey and the honeycomb.

PSALM 19:7–8, 10

This Book of the Law shall not depart from your
mouth, but you shall meditate in it day and night,
that you may observe to do according to all that is
written in it. For then you will make your way prosperous, and then you will have good success.

JOSHUA 1:8

*God's Promises*

I will meditate on Your precepts,
And contemplate Your ways.
I will delight myself in Your statutes;
I will not forget Your word.

PSALM 119:15–16

You put off, concerning your former conduct, the old man which grows corrupt according to the deceitful lusts, and be renewed in the spirit of your mind, and that you put on the new man which was created according to God, in true righteousness and holiness.

EPHESIANS 4:22–24

We do not lose heart. Even though our outward man is perishing, yet the inward man is being renewed day by day.

2 CORINTHIANS 4:16

The LORD will command His lovingkindness
    in the daytime,
And in the night His song shall be
    with me—
A prayer to the God of my life.

PSALM 42:8

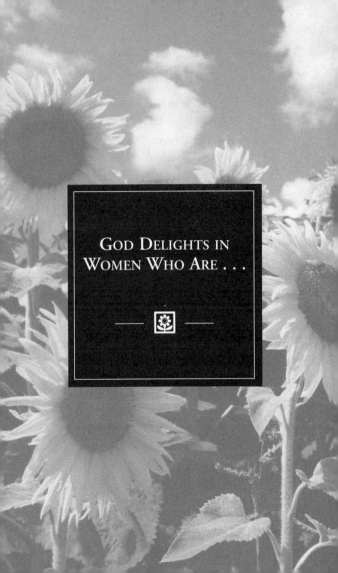

GOD DELIGHTS IN
WOMEN WHO ARE . . .

When my father and my mother forsake me,
Then the LORD will take care of me.

PSALM 27:10

O God, You are my God;
Early will I seek You;
My soul thirsts for You;
My flesh longs for You
In a dry and thirsty land
Where there is no water.

PSALM 63:1

Seek the LORD and His strength;
Seek His face evermore!
Remember His marvelous works which
     He has done,
His wonders, and the judgments of
     His mouth.

1 CHRONICLES 16:11–12

*God's Promises*

If you confess with your mouth the Lord Jesus and believe in your heart that God has raised Him from the dead, you will be saved.

ROMANS 10:9

> I love those who love me,
> And those who seek me diligently will
>     find me.

PROVERBS 8:17

Till I come, give attention to reading, to exhortation, to doctrine.

1 TIMOTHY 4:13

> There is a way that seems right to a man,
> But its end is the way of death.

PROVERBS 14:12

> I sought the LORD, and He heard me,
> And delivered me from all my fears.

PSALM 34:4

Always pursue what is good both for yourselves and for all.

1 THESSSALONIANS 5:15

I will not leave you orphans; I will come to you.

JOHN 14:18

I thank my God upon every remembrance of you.

PHILIPPIANS 1:3

In You, O LORD, I put my trust;
Let me never be put to shame.
Deliver me in Your righteousness, and
    cause me to escape;
Incline Your ear to me, and save me.
For You are my hope, O Lord GOD;
You are my trust from my youth.

PSALM 71:1– 2, 5

It is better to trust in the LORD
Than to put confidence in man.

PSALM 118:8

With men this is impossible, but with God all things
are possible.

MATTHEW 19:26

The LORD shall preserve you from all evil;
He shall preserve your soul.
The LORD shall preserve your going out
    and your coming in
From this time forth, and even forevermore.

PSALM 121:7–8

Therefore submit to God. Resist the devil and he will flee from you.

JAMES 4:7

Grace and peace be multiplied to you in the knowledge of God and of Jesus our Lord, as His divine power has given to us all things that pertain to life and godliness, through the knowledge of Him who called us by glory and virtue, by which have been given to us exceedingly great and precious promises, that through these you may be partakers of the divine nature, having escaped the corruption that is in the world through lust.

2 PETER 1:2–4

Who is he who overcomes the world, but he who believes that Jesus is the Son of God?

1 JOHN 5:5

Now to Him who is able to keep you
from stumbling,
And to present you faultless
Before the presence of His glory with
exceeding joy,
To God our Savior,
Who alone is wise,
Be glory and majesty,
Dominion and power,
Both now and forever.

JUDE 24–25

There is therefore now no condemnation to those who are in Christ Jesus, who do not walk according to the flesh, but according to the Spirit. For the law of the Spirit of life in Christ Jesus has made me free from the law of sin and death.

ROMANS 8:1–2

If we confess our sins, He is faithful and just to forgive us our sins and to cleanse us from all unrighteousness.

1 JOHN 1:9

You have forgiven the iniquity of
      Your people;
You have covered all their sin.

PSALM 85:2

The Lord is faithful, who will establish you and guard you from the evil one.

2 THESSALONIANS 3:3

Now whom you forgive anything, I also forgive. For if indeed I have forgiven anything, I have forgiven that one for your sakes in the presence of Christ, lest Satan should take advantage of us; for we are not ignorant of his devices.

2 CORINTHIANS 2:10–11

To him who overcomes I will grant to sit with Me on My throne, as I also overcame and sat down with My Father on His throne.

REVELATION 3:21

The Lord will deliver me from every evil work and preserve me for His heavenly kingdom. To Him be glory forever and ever. Amen!

2 TIMOTHY 4:18

I will instruct you and teach you in the
way you should go;
I will guide you with My eye.

PSALM 32:8

This Book of the Law shall not depart from your
mouth, but you shall meditate in it day and night, that
you may observe to do according to all that is written in
it. For then you will make your way prosperous, and
then you will have good success.

JOSHUA 1:8

That we should no longer be children, tossed to and
fro and carried about with every wind of doctrine, by
the trickery of men, in the cunning craftiness of
deceitful plotting, but, speaking the truth in love,
may grow up in all things into Him who is the
head—Christ.

EPHESIANS 4:14–15

Be doers of the word, and not hearers only, deceiving
yourselves.

JAMES 1:22

I am the vine, you are the branches. He who abides in Me, and I in him, bears much fruit; for without Me you can do nothing.

JOHN 15:5

O God, You are my God;
Early will I seek You;
My soul thirsts for You;
My flesh longs for You
In a dry and thirsty land
Where there is no water.
So I have looked for You in the sanctuary,
To see Your power and Your glory.
My soul shall be satisfied as with marrow
        and fatness,
And my mouth shall praise You with
        joyful lips.
When I remember You on my bed,
I meditate on You in the night watches.
Because You have been my help,
Therefore in the shadow of Your wings I
        will rejoice.

PSALM 63:1–2, 5–7

You did not choose Me, but I chose you and appointed you that you should go and bear fruit, and that your fruit should remain, that whatever you ask the Father in My name He may give you.

JOHN 15:16

For in Him we live and move and have our being, as also some of your own poets have said, "For we are also His offspring."

ACTS 17:28

# GOD DELIGHTS IN WOMEN WHO ARE . . .
## SERVING HIM

If it seems evil to you to serve the LORD, choose for yourselves this day whom you will serve, whether the gods which your fathers served that were on the other side of the River, or the gods of the Amorites, in whose land you dwell. But as for me and my house, we will serve the LORD.

JOSHUA 24:15

If anyone serves Me, let him follow Me; and where I am, there My servant will be also. If anyone serves Me, him My Father will honor.

JOHN 12:26

Then Jesus said to him, "Away with you, Satan! For it is written, 'You shall worship the LORD your God, and Him only you shall serve.'"

MATTHEW 4:10

So the people asked him, saying, "What shall we do then?"

He answered and said to them, "He who has two tunics, let him give to him who has none; and he who has food, let him do likewise."

LUKE 3:10–11

By this all will know that you are My disciples, if you have love for one another.

JOHN 13:35

Command those who are rich in this present age not to be haughty, nor to trust in uncertain riches but in the living God, who gives us richly all things to enjoy. Let them do good, that they be rich in good works, ready to give, willing to share, storing up for themselves a good foundation for the time to come, that they may lay hold on eternal life.

1 TIMOTHY 6:17–19

Let each one examine his own work, and then he will have rejoicing in himself alone, and not in another. For each one shall bear his own load.

Let him who is taught the word share in all good things with him who teaches.

Let us not grow weary while doing good, for in due season we shall reap if we do not lose heart.

GALATIANS 6:4–6, 9

The people said to Joshua, "The LORD our God we will serve, and His voice we will obey!"

JOSHUA 24:24

Now by this we know that we know Him, if we keep His commandments.

Whoever keeps His word, truly the love of God is perfected in him. By this we know that we are in Him.

1 JOHN 2:3, 5

Having been justified by faith, we have peace with God through our Lord Jesus Christ, through whom also we have access by faith into this grace in which we stand, and rejoice in hope of the glory of God. And not only that, but we also glory in tribulations, knowing that tribulation produces perseverance; and perseverance, character; and character, hope.

ROMANS 5:1–4

Finally, my brethren, be strong in the Lord and in the power of His might. Put on the whole armor of God, that you may be able to stand against the wiles of the devil.

EPHESIANS 6:10–11

That which we have seen and heard we declare to you, that you also may have fellowship with us; and truly our fellowship is with the Father and with His Son Jesus Christ.

1 JOHN 1:3

Someone will say, "You have faith, and I have works." Show me your faith without your works, and I will show you my faith by my works.

Do you see that faith was working together with his works, and by works faith was made perfect?

JAMES 2:18, 22

"Woe to the rebellious children," says the
    LORD,
"Who take counsel, but not of Me,
  And who devise plans, but not of My Spirit,
  That they may add sin to sin.

ISAIAH 30:1

Though now you do not see Him, yet believing, you rejoice with joy inexpressible and full of glory.

1 PETER 1:18

My beloved brethren, let every man be swift to hear, slow to speak, slow to wrath; for the wrath of man does not produce the righteousness of God.

Therefore lay aside all filthiness and overflow of wickedness, and receive with meekness the implanted word, which is able to save your souls.

Pure and undefiled religion before God and the Father is this: to visit orphans and widows in their trouble, and to keep oneself unspotted from the world.

JAMES 1:19–21, 27

Now these are the ones sown among thorns; they are the ones who hear the word, and the cares of this world, the deceitfulness of riches, and the desires for other things entering in choke the word, and it becomes unfruitful. But these are the ones sown on good ground, those who hear the word, accept it, and bear fruit: some thirtyfold, some sixty, and some a hundred.

MARK 4:18–20

We speak, not as pleasing men, but who tests our hearts.

1 THESSALONIANS 2:4

GOD WALKS WITH
WOMEN . . .

He heals the brokenhearted
And binds up their wounds.

PSALM 147:3

A man's heart plans his way,
But the LORD directs his steps.
The lot is cast into the lap,
But its every decision is from the LORD.

PROVERBS 16:9, 33

The LORD is near to those who have a
    broken heart,
And saves such as have a contrite spirit.
Many are the afflictions of the righteous,
But the LORD delivers him out of them all.

PSALM 34:18–19

Come to Me, all you who labor and are heavy laden,
and I will give you rest. Take My yoke upon you and
learn from Me, for I am gentle and lowly in heart,
and you will find rest for your souls.

MATTHEW 11:28–29

"Now I will rise," says the LORD;
"Now I will be exalted,
Now I will lift Myself up."

ISAIAH 33:10

The LORD also will be a refuge for
        the oppressed,
A refuge in times of trouble.
And those who know Your name will
        put their trust in You;
For You, LORD, have not forsaken those
        who seek You.

PSALM 9:9–10

In the day when I cried out, You
        answered me,
And made me bold with strength in my soul.

PSALM 138:3

The LORD will guide you continually,
And satisfy your soul in drought,
And strengthen your bones;
You shall be like a watered garden,
And like a spring of water, whose waters
        do not fail.

ISAIAH 58:11

The fear of man brings a snare,
But whoever trusts in the LORD shall be safe.

PROVERBS 29:25

Through God we will do valiantly,
For it is He who shall tread down our enemies.

PSALM 60:12

Beloved, do not think it strange concerning the fiery trial which is to try you, as though some strange thing happened to you; but rejoice to the extent that you partake of Christ's sufferings, that when His glory is revealed, you may also be glad with exceeding joy.

1 PETER 4:12–13

Yes, may you see your children's children.
Peace be upon Israel!

PSALM 128:6

Now thanks be to God who always leads us in triumph in Christ, and through us diffuses the fragrance of His knowledge in every place.

2 CORINTHIANS 2:14

> My heart is steadfast, O God, my heart
>      is steadfast;
> I will sing and give praise.

PSALM 57:7

He said to me, "My grace is sufficient for you, for My strength is made perfect in weakness." Therefore most gladly I will rather boast in my infirmities, that the power of Christ may rest upon me.

2 CORINTHIANS 12:9

> The LORD will perfect that which
>      concerns me;
> Your mercy, O LORD, endures forever;
> Do not forsake the works of Your hands.

PSALM 138:8

My soul, wait silently for God alone,
For my expectation is from Him.
He only is my rock and my salvation;
He is my defense;
I shall not be moved.
In God is my salvation and my glory;
The rock of my strength,
And my refuge, is in God.

PSALM 62:5–7

When you pass through the waters, I will
    be with you;
And through the rivers, they shall not
    overflow you.
When you walk through the fire, you
    shall not be burned,
Nor shall the flame scorch you.

ISAIAH 43:2

Keep me as the apple of Your eye;
Hide me under the shadow of Your wings.

PSALM 17:8

Yea, though I walk through the valley of
    the shadow of death,
I will fear no evil;
For You are with me;
Your rod and Your staff, they comfort me.

PSALM 23:4

You number my wanderings;
Put my tears into Your bottle;
Are they not in Your book?
In God I have put my trust;
I will not be afraid.
What can man do to me?

PSALM 56:8, 11

He raises the poor out of the dust,
And lifts the needy out of the ash heap,
He grants the barren woman a home,
Like a joyful mother of children.
Praise the LORD!

PSALM 113:7, 9

For in the time of trouble
He shall hide me in His pavilion;
In the secret place of His tabernacle
He shall hide me;
He shall set me high upon a rock.

PSALM 27:5

Do not be a terror to me;
You are my hope in the day of doom.

JEREMIAH 17:17

My soul waits for the Lord
More than those who watch for the
      morning—
Yes, more than those who watch for
      the morning.

PSALM 130:6

My brethren, count it all joy when you fall into various trials, knowing that the testing of your faith produces patience. But let patience have its perfect work, that you may be perfect and complete, lacking nothing.

JAMES 1:2–4

Be patient, brethren, until the coming of the Lord. See how the farmer waits for the precious fruit of the earth, waiting patiently for it until it receives the early and latter rain. You also be patient. Establish your hearts, for the coming of the Lord is at hand.

JAMES 5:7–8

He said, "My Presence will go with you, and I will give you rest."

EXODUS 33:14

Wait on the LORD;
Be of good courage,
And He shall strengthen your heart;
Wait, I say, on the LORD!

PSALM 27:14

Those who wait on the LORD
Shall renew their strength;
They shall mount up with wings like eagles,
They shall run and not be weary,
They shall walk and not faint.

ISAIAH 40:31

I cried to the LORD with my voice,
And He heard me from His holy hill.
I lay down and slept;
I awoke, for the LORD sustained me.

PSALM 3:4–5

So, after he had patiently endured, he obtained the promise.

HEBREWS 6:15

LORD, I cry out to You;
Make haste to me!
Give ear to my voice when I cry out to You.
Let my prayer be set before You as incense,
The lifting up of my hands as the evening
    sacrifice.

PSALM 141:1–2

Many people shall come and say,
"Come, and let us go up to the mountain
    of the LORD,
To the house of the God of Jacob;
He will teach us His ways,
And we shall walk in His paths."
For out of Zion shall go forth the law,
And the word of the LORD from Jerusalem.

ISAIAH 2:3

Fight the good fight of faith, lay hold on eternal life,
to which you were also called and have confessed the
good confession in the presence of many witnesses.

1 TIMOTHY 6:12

Though He was a Son, yet He learned obedience by the things which He suffered.

HEBREWS 5:8

I have fought the good fight, I have finished the race, I have kept the faith. Finally, there is laid up for me the crown of righteousness, which the Lord, the righteous Judge, will give to me on that Day, and not to me only but also to all who have loved His appearing.

2 TIMOTHY 4:7–8

Now godliness with contentment is great gain. For we brought nothing into this world, and it is certain we can carry nothing out. And having food and clothing, with these we shall be content.

1 TIMOTHY 6:6–8

> I know that whatever God does,
> It shall be forever.
> Nothing can be added to it,
> And nothing taken from it.
> God does it, that men should fear before
>     Him.

ECCLESIASTES 3:14

*God's Promises*

The wisdom that is from above is first pure, then peaceable, gentle, willing to yield, full of mercy and good fruits, without partiality and without hypocrisy.

JAMES 3:17

For this is commendable, if because of conscience toward God one endures grief, suffering wrongfully. For what credit is it if, when you are beaten for your faults, you take it patiently? But when you do good and suffer, if you take it patiently, this is commendable before God.

1 PETER 2:19–20

May our Lord Jesus Christ . . . comfort your hearts and establish you in every good word and work.

2 THESSALONIANS 2:16

Love bears all things, believes all things, hopes all things, endures all things.

1 CORINTHIANS 13:7

He who loves his life will lose it, and he who hates his life in this world will keep it for eternal life.

JOHN 12:25

Set your mind on things above, not on things on the earth.

COLOSSIANS 3:2

Command those who are rich in this present age not to be haughty, nor to trust in uncertain riches but in the living God, who gives us richly all things to enjoy. Let them do good, that they be rich in good works, ready to give, willing to share, storing up for themselves a good foundation for the time to come, that they may lay hold on eternal life.

1 TIMOTHY 6:17–19

Listen to counsel and receive instruction,
That you may be wise in your latter days.

PROVERBS 19:20

For I considered all this in my heart, so that I could declare it all: that the righteous and the wise and their works are in the hand of God. People know neither love nor hatred by anything they see before them.

ECCLESIASTES 9:1


You are a chosen generation, a royal priesthood, a holy nation, His own special people, that you may proclaim the praises of Him who called you out of darkness into His marvelous light.

1 PETER 2:9


He has not dealt with us according to
    our sins,
Nor punished us according to our iniquities.
For as the heavens are high above the earth,
So great is His mercy toward those who
    fear Him;
As far as the east is from the west,
So far has He removed our transgressions
    from us.

PSALM 103:10–12


Cast your burden on the LORD,
And He shall sustain you;
He shall never permit the righteous to
    be moved.

PSALM 55:22

GOD ENCOURAGES
EACH WOMAN TO . . .

Let brotherly love continue. Do not forget to entertain strangers, for by so doing some have unwittingly entertained angels.

HEBREWS 13:1–2

A friend loves at all times,
And a brother is born for adversity.

PROVERBS 17:17

This is My commandment, that you love one another as I have loved you. Greater love has no one than this, than to lay down one's life for his friends.

JOHN 15:12–13

If one member suffers, all the members suffer with it; or if one member is honored, all the members rejoice with it.

1 CORINTHIANS 12:26

Two are better than one,
Because they have a good reward for
their labor.

ECCLESIASTES 4:9

*God's Promises*

Everyone helped his neighbor,
And said to his brother,
"Be of good courage!"

ISAIAH 41:6

For whoever does the will of My Father in heaven is
My brother and sister and mother.

MATTHEW 12:50

For as the body is one and has many members, but all
the members of that one body, being many, are one
body, so also is Christ.

1 CORINTHIANS 12:12

Through love, serve one another.

GALATIANS 5:13

Let all that you do be done with love.

1 CORINTHIANS 16:14

Let us not grow weary while doing good, for in due season we shall reap if we do not lose heart.

GALATIANS 6:9

Give, and it will be given to you: good measure, pressed down, shaken together, and running over will be put into your bosom. For with the same measure that you use, it will be measured back to you.

LUKE 6:38

She extends her hand to the poor,
Yes, she reaches out her hands to the needy.

PROVERBS 31:20

He who gives to the poor will not lack,
But he who hides his eyes will have
      many curses.

PROVERBS 28:27

Defend the poor and fatherless;
Do justice to the afflicted and needy.
Deliver the poor and needy;
Free them from the hand of the wicked.

PSALM 82:3–4

By this we know love, because He laid down His life for us. And we also ought to lay down our lives for the brethren. But whoever has this world's goods, and sees his brother in need, and shuts up his heart from him, how does the love of God abide in him?

1 JOHN 3:16–17

Whoever gives one of these little ones only a cup of cold water in the name of a disciple, assuredly, I say to you, he shall by no means lose his reward.

MATTHEW 10:42

What does the LORD require of you but to do justly, to love mercy, and to walk humbly with your God?

MICAH 6:8

Be tenderhearted, be courteous . . . that you may inherit a blessing.

1 PETER 3:9

He who does not love does not know God, for God
is love.

1 JOHN 4:8

Now, little children, abide in Him, that when He
appears, we may have confidence and not be ashamed
before Him at His coming.

1 JOHN 2:28

A new commandment I give to you, that you love one
another; as I have loved you, that you also love one
another. By this all will know that you are My disciples, if you have love for one another.

JOHN 13:34–35

Whoever desires to be first among you, let him be
your slave—just as the Son of Man did not come to
be served, but to serve, and to give His life a ransom
for many.

MATTHEW 20:27–28

For you, brethren, have been called to liberty; only do not use liberty as an opportunity for the flesh, but through love serve one another.

GALATIANS 5:13

As each one has received a gift, minister it to one another, as good stewards of the manifold grace of God. If anyone speaks, let him speak as the oracles of God. If anyone ministers, let him do it as with the ability which God supplies, that in all things God may be glorified through Jesus Christ, to whom belong the glory and the dominion forever and ever.

1 PETER 4:10–11

Whatever you do, do it heartily, as to the Lord and not to men, knowing that from the Lord you will receive the reward of the inheritance; for you serve the Lord Christ. But he who does wrong will be repaid for what he has done, and there is no partiality.

COLOSSIANS 3:23–25

He who is faithful in what is least is faithful also in much; and he who is unjust in what is least is unjust also in much. Therefore if you have not been faithful in the unrighteous mammon, who will commit to your trust the true riches? And if you have not been faithful in what is another man's, who will give you what is your own?

No servant can serve two masters; for either he will hate the one and love the other, or else he will be loyal to the one and despise the other. You cannot serve God and mammon.

LUKE 16:10–13

Rejoice with those who rejoice, and weep with those who weep. Be of the same mind toward one another. Do not set your mind on high things, but associate with the humble. Do not be wise in your own opinion.

ROMANS 12:15–16

Therefore comfort each other and edify one another, just as you also are doing.

1 THESSALONIANS 5:11

Therefore let us pursue the things which make for peace and the things by which one may edify another.

ROMANS 14:19

Let us consider one another in order to stir up love and good works, not forsaking the assembling of ourselves together, as is the manner of some, but exhorting one another, and so much the more as you see the Day approaching.

HEBREWS 10:24–25

If we walk in the light as He is in the light, we have fellowship with one another, and the blood of Jesus Christ His Son cleanses us from all sin.

1 JOHN 1:7

If then you were raised with Christ, seek those things which are above, where Christ is, sitting at the right hand of God. Set your mind on things above, not on things on the earth.

COLOSSIANS 3:1–2

You are my hiding place;
You shall preserve me from trouble;
You shall surround me with songs of
deliverance.

PSALM 32:7

Do not fear, little flock, for it is your Father's good pleasure to give you the kingdom.

LUKE 12:32

May the Lord of peace Himself give you peace always in every way.

2 THESSALONIANS 3:16

God has sent His only begotten Son into the world, that we might live through Him.

1 JOHN 4:9

Behold, I am the LORD, the God of all flesh. Is there anything too hard for Me?

JEREMIAH 32:27

Let this mind be in you which was also in Christ Jesus.

PHILIPPIANS 2:5

> For the eyes of the LORD are on the
>     righteous,
> And His ears are open to their prayers;
> But the face of the LORD is against those
>     who do evil.
> And who is he who will harm you if you
become followers of what is good?

1 PETER 3:12–13

Take the helmet of salvation, and the sword of the Spirit, which is the word of God; praying always with all prayer and supplication in the Spirit, being watchful to this end with all perseverance and supplication for all the saints.

EPHESIANS 6:17–18

You are of God, little children, and have overcome them, because He who is in you is greater than he who is in the world.

1 JOHN 4:4

Depart from me, all you workers of iniquity;
For the LORD has heard the voice of
    my weeping.
The LORD has heard my supplication;
The LORD will receive my prayer.

PSALM 6:8–9

Give ear, O LORD, to my prayer;
And attend to the voice of my supplications.
In the day of my trouble I will call upon You,
For You will answer me.

PSALM 86:6–7

Now this is the confidence that we have in Him, that if we ask anything according to His will, He hears us. And if we know that He hears us, whatever we ask, we know that we have the petitions that we have asked of Him.

1 John 5:14–15

Rejoice always, pray without ceasing, in everything give thanks; for this is the will of God in Christ Jesus for you.

1 THESSALONIANS 5:16–18

GOD ENCOURAGES EACH WOMAN TO . . .
CELEBRATE WITH JOY

I will praise You, O LORD, with my
    whole heart;
I will tell of all Your marvelous works.
I will be glad and rejoice in You;
I will sing praise to Your name,
    O Most High.

PSALM 9:1–2

It will be said in that day:
"Behold, this is our God;
We have waited for Him, and He will save us.
This is the LORD;
We have waited for Him;
We will be glad and rejoice in His salvation."

ISAIAH 25:9

I will sing of the mercies of the LORD forever;
With my mouth will I make known
    Your faithfulness to all generations.

PSALM 89:1

Blessed are the people who know the joyful sound!

PSALM 89:15

I will delight myself in Your statutes;
I will not forget Your word.
Make me understand the way of Your precepts;
So shall I meditate on Your wonderful works.

PSALM 119:16, 27


A merry heart makes a cheerful countenance,
But by sorrow of the heart the spirit is broken.

PROVERBS 15:13


Thus says the LORD: "Again there shall be heard in this place—of which you say, 'It is desolate, without man and without beast'—in the cities of Judah, in the streets of Jerusalem that are desolate, without man and without inhabitant and without beast, the voice of joy and the voice of gladness, the voice of the bridegroom and the voice of the bride, the voice of those who will say:

'Praise the Lord of hosts,
For the Lord is good,
For His mercy endures forever'—

and of those who will bring the sacrifice of praise into the house of the LORD. For I will cause the captives of the land to return as at the first," says the LORD.

JEREMIAH 33:10–11

King Hezekiah and the leaders commanded the Levites
to sing praise to the LORD with the words of David and
of Asaph the seer. So they sang praises with gladness,
and they bowed their heads and worshiped.

2 CHRONICLES 29:30


The LORD your God in your midst,
The Mighty One, will save;
He will rejoice over you with gladness,
He will quiet you with His love,
He will rejoice over you with singing.

ZEPHANIAH 3:17


Let them shout for joy and be glad,
Who favor my righteous cause;
And let them say continually,
"Let the LORD be magnified,
Who has pleasure in the prosperity of
    His servant."
And my tongue shall speak of Your
    righteousness
And of Your praise all the day long.

PSALM 35:27–28


Bow down Your heavens, O LORD, and
    come down;
Touch the mountains, and they shall smoke.

PSALM 144:5

GOD TEACHES A
WOMAN HOW TO . . .

Beloved, do not believe every spirit, but test the spirits, whether they are of God; because many false prophets have gone out into the world.

1 John 4:1

> The LORD is your keeper;
> The LORD is your shade at your right hand.
> The LORD shall preserve you from all evil;
> He shall preserve your soul.
> The LORD shall preserve your going out
>    and your coming in
> From this time forth, and even forevermore.

Psalm 121:5, 7–8

We have such trust through Christ toward God. Not that we are sufficient of ourselves to think of anything as being from ourselves, but our sufficiency is from God.

2 Corinthians 3:4–5

When I saw Him, I fell at His feet as dead. But He laid
His right hand on me, saying to me, "Do not be afraid;
I am the First and the Last. I am He who lives, and was
dead, and behold, I am alive forevermore. Amen. And
I have the keys of Hades and of Death."

REVELATION 1:17–18

> The LORD is my shepherd;
> I shall not want.
> He makes me to lie down in green pastures;
> He leads me beside the still waters.
> He restores my soul;
> He leads me in the paths of righteousness
> For His name's sake.
> Yea, though I walk through the valley of
>     the shadow of death,
> I will fear no evil;
> For You are with me;
> Your rod and Your staff, they comfort me.

PSALM 23:1–4

> My help comes from the LORD,
> Who made heaven and earth.
> He will not allow your foot to be moved;
> He who keeps you will not slumber.

PSALM 121:2–3

*God's Promises*

I will say of the LORD, "He is my refuge
    and my fortress;
My God, in Him I will trust."
Surely He shall deliver you from the snare
    of the fowler
And from the perilous pestilence.
He shall cover you with His feathers,
And under His wings you shall take refuge;
His truth shall be your shield and buckler.

PSALM 91:2–4

For there are three that bear witness in heaven: the Father, the Word, and the Holy Spirit; and these three are one.

1 JOHN 5:7

Let us hold fast the confession of our hope without wavering, for He who promised is faithful.

HEBREWS 10:23

Have I not commanded you? Be strong and of good courage; do not be afraid, nor be dismayed, for the LORD your God is with you wherever you go.

JOSHUA 1:9

For with God nothing will be impossible.

LUKE 1:37

Beloved, while I was very diligent to write to you concerning our common salvation, I found it necessary to write to you exhorting you to contend earnestly for the faith which was once for all delivered to the saints.

JUDE 3

For we walk by faith, not by sight.

2 CORINTHIANS 5:7

Having shod your feet with the preparation of the gospel of peace; above all, taking the shield of faith with which you will be able to quench all the fiery darts of the wicked one.

EPHESIANS 6:15–16

You, beloved, building yourselves up on your most holy faith, praying in the Holy Spirit, keep yourselves in the love of God, looking for the mercy of our Lord Jesus Christ unto eternal life.

JUDE 20–21

Be steadfast, immovable, always abounding in the work of the Lord.

1 CORINTHIANS 15:58

To Him who is able to keep you from stumbling . . . be glory and majesty.

JUDE 24 –25

I say to you that likewise there will be more joy in heaven over one sinner who repents than over ninety-nine just persons who need no repentance.

LUKE 15:7

This is the day the LORD has made;
We will rejoice and be glad in it.

PSALM 118:24

These things I have spoken to you, that My joy may remain in you, and that your joy may be full. This is My commandment, that you love one another as I have loved you.

JOHN 15:11–12

Create in me a clean heart, O God,
And renew a steadfast spirit within me.
Do not cast me away from Your presence,
And do not take Your Holy Spirit from me.
Restore to me the joy of Your salvation,
And uphold me by Your generous Spirit.

PSALM 51:10–12

Let us come before His presence
    with thanksgiving;
Let us shout joyfully to Him with psalms.

PSALM 95:2

Because Your lovingkindness is better
    than life,
My lips shall praise You.
Thus I will bless You while I live;
I will lift up my hands in Your name.
My soul shall be satisfied as with marrow
    and fatness,
And my mouth shall praise You with
    joyful lips.

PSALM 63:3–5

The kingdom of God is not eating and drinking, but
righteousness and peace and joy in the Holy Spirit.

ROMANS 14:17

A merry heart makes a cheerful countenance,
But by sorrow of the heart the spirit is
    broken.

PROVERBS 15:13

Oh, satisfy us early with Your mercy, that we may
rejoice and be glad all our days!

PSALM 90:14

Behold, all those who were incensed
        against you
Shall be ashamed and disgraced;
They shall be as nothing,
And those who strive with you shall perish.
You shall seek them and not find them—
Those who contended with you.
Those who war against you
Shall be as nothing,
As a nonexistent thing.
For I, the LORD your God, will hold
        your right hand,
Saying to you, "Fear not, I will help you."

ISAIAH 41:11–13


Let the word of Christ dwell in you richly in all wisdom, teaching and admonishing one another in psalms and hymns and spiritual songs, singing with grace in your hearts to the Lord.

COLOSSIANS 3:16

There is therefore now no condemnation to those who are in Christ Jesus, who do not walk according to the flesh, but according to the Spirit. For the law of the Spirit of life in Christ Jesus has made me free from the law of sin and death.

ROMANS 8:1–2

I sought the LORD, and He heard me,
And delivered me from all my fears.

PSALM 34:4

I will sing to the LORD as long as I live;
I will sing praise to my God while I have
    my being.
May my meditation be sweet to Him;
I will be glad in the LORD.

PSALM 104:33–34

Teaching us that, denying ungodliness and worldly lusts, we should live soberly, righteously, and godly in the present age, looking for the blessed hope and glorious appearing of our great God and Savior Jesus Christ.

TITUS 2:12–13

I have been crucified with Christ; it is no longer I who live, but Christ lives in me; and the life which I now live in the flesh I live by faith in the Son of God, who loved me and gave Himself for me.

GALATIANS 2:20

My voice You shall hear in the morning,
    O LORD;
In the morning I will direct it to You,
And I will look up.

PSALM 5:3

The LORD is my light and my salvation;
Whom shall I fear?
The LORD is the strength of my life;
Of whom shall I be afraid?
When the wicked came against me
To eat up my flesh,
My enemies and foes,
They stumbled and fell.
Though an army may encamp against me,
My heart shall not fear;
Though war may rise against me,
In this I will be confident.
One thing I have desired of the LORD,
That will I seek:
That I may dwell in the house of the LORD
All the days of my life,
To behold the beauty of the LORD,
And to inquire in His temple.
For in the time of trouble
He shall hide me in His pavilion;
In the secret place of His tabernacle
He shall hide me;
He shall set me high upon a rock.

PSALM 27:1–5

Whoever listens to me will dwell safely,
And will be secure, without fear of evil.

PROVERBS 1:33

I cry out to the LORD with my voice;
With my voice to the LORD I make my
    supplication.
I pour out my complaint before Him;
I declare before Him my trouble.

PSALM 142:1–2

The LORD is your keeper;
The LORD is your shade at your right hand.
The sun shall not strike you by day,
Nor the moon by night.
The LORD shall preserve you from all evil;
He shall preserve your soul.
The LORD shall preserve your going out
    and your coming in
From this time forth, and even forevermore.

PSALM 121:5–8

May He send you help from the sanctuary,
And strengthen you out of Zion.

PSALM 20:2

You alone, O LORD, make me dwell in safety.

PSALM 4:8

"No weapon formed against you shall prosper,
And every tongue which rises against you
      in judgment
You shall condemn.
This is the heritage of the servants of
      the LORD,
And their righteousness is from Me,"
Says the LORD.

ISAIAH 54:17

I will both lie down in peace, and sleep;
For You alone, O LORD, make me dwell
      in safety.

PSALM 4:8

When you pass through the waters, I will
      be with you;
And through the rivers, they shall not
      overflow you.
When you walk through the fire, you
      shall not be burned,
Nor shall the flame scorch you.

ISAIAH 43:2

The Lord is faithful, who will establish you and guard
you from the evil one.

2 THESSALONIANS 3:3

Now this is the confidence that we have in Him, that if
we ask anything according to His will, He hears us. And
if we know that He hears us, whatever we ask, we know
that we have the petitions that we have asked of Him.

1 JOHN 5:14–15

If you diligently heed the voice of the LORD your
God and do what is right in His sight, give ear to His
commandments and keep all His statutes, I will put
none of the diseases on you which I have brought on
the Egyptians. For I am the LORD who heals you.

EXODUS 15:26

Seek first the kingdom of God and His righteousness,
and all these things shall be added to you.

MATTHEW 6:33

Do not become sluggish, but imitate those who
through faith and patience inherit the promises.

HEBREWS 6:12

Let us hold fast the confession of our hope without
wavering, for He who promised is faithful.

HEBREWS 10:23

By which have been given to us exceedingly great and precious promises, that through these you may be partakers of the divine nature, having escaped the corruption that is in the world through lust.

But also for this very reason, giving all diligence, add to your faith virtue, to virtue knowledge, to knowledge self-control, to self-control perseverance, to perseverance godliness, to godliness brotherly kindness, and to brotherly kindness love. For if these things are yours and abound, you will be neither barren nor unfruitful in the knowledge of our Lord Jesus Christ.

2 PETER 1:4–8

Now faith is the substance of things hoped for, the evidence of things not seen.

Without faith it is impossible to please Him, for he who comes to God must believe that He is, and that He is a rewarder of those who diligently seek Him.

By faith Sarah herself also received strength to conceive seed, and she bore a child when she was past the age, because she judged Him faithful who had promised.

HEBREWS 11:1, 6, 11

For with God nothing will be impossible.

LUKE 1:37

GOD BLESSES
WOMEN WHEN
THEY . . .

In the LORD I put my trust;
How can you say to my soul,
"Flee as a bird to your mountain"?
For look! The wicked bend their bow,
They make ready their arrow on the string,
That they may shoot secretly at the upright
    in heart.
If the foundations are destroyed,
What can the righteous do?
The LORD is in His holy temple,
The LORD's throne is in heaven;
His eyes behold,
His eyelids test the sons of men.
The LORD tests the righteous,
But the wicked and the one who loves
    violence His soul hates.
Upon the wicked He will rain coals;
Fire and brimstone and a burning wind
Shall be the portion of their cup.
For the LORD is righteous,
He loves righteousness;
His countenance beholds the upright.

PSALM 11:1–7

*God's Promises*

Trust in Him at all times, you people;
Pour out your heart before Him;
God is a refuge for us.

PSALM 62:8

Those who trust in the LORD
Are like Mount Zion,
Which cannot be moved, but abides forever.
As the mountains surround Jerusalem,
So the LORD surrounds His people
From this time forth and forever.
For the scepter of wickedness shall not rest
On the land allotted to the righteous,
Lest the righteous reach out their hands
    to iniquity.
Do good, O LORD, to those who are good,
And to those who are upright in their hearts.
As for such as turn aside to their crooked
    ways,
The LORD shall lead them away
With the workers of iniquity.
Peace be upon Israel!

PSALM 125:1–5

For You will light my lamp;
The LORD my God will enlighten my darkness.
For by You I can run against a troop,
By my God I can leap over a wall.
As for God, His way is perfect;
The word of the LORD is proven;
He is a shield to all who trust in Him.

PSALM 18:28–30


Whenever I am afraid,
I will trust in You.
In God (I will praise His word),
In God I have put my trust;
I will not fear.
What can flesh do to me?

PSALM 56:3–4


In God I have put my trust;
I will not be afraid.
What can man do to me?
Vows made to You are binding upon me,
    O God;
I will render praises to You.

PSALM 56:11–12


He shall cover you with His feathers, and under His
wings you shall take refuge.

PSALM 91:4

But You are holy,
Enthroned in the praises of Israel.
Our fathers trusted in You;
They trusted, and You delivered them.

PSALM 22:3–4

LORD, how they have increased who
     trouble me!
Many are they who rise up against me.
Many are they who say of me,
"There is no help for him in God."
But You, O LORD, are a shield for me,
My glory and the One who lifts up my head.
I cried to the LORD with my voice,
And He heard me from His holy hill.
I lay down and slept;
I awoke, for the LORD sustained me.
I will not be afraid of ten thousands of people
Who have set themselves against me all around.
Arise, O LORD;
Save me, O my God!
For You have struck all my enemies on
     the cheekbone;
You have broken the teeth of the ungodly.
Salvation belongs to the LORD.
Your blessing is upon Your people.

PSALM 3:1–8

Let the saints be joyful in glory;
Let them sing aloud on their beds.
Let the high praises of God be in
    their mouth,
And a two-edged sword in their hand.

PSALM 149:5–6


My heart is steadfast, O God, my heart
    is steadfast;
I will sing and give praise.
Awake, my glory!
Awake, lute and harp!
I will awaken the dawn.
I will praise You, O Lord, among the peoples;
I will sing to You among the nations.

PSALM 57:7–9


Praise Him with loud cymbals;
Praise Him with clashing cymbals!
Let everything that has breath praise
    the LORD.
Praise the LORD!

PSALM 150:5–6

Because Your lovingkindness is better than life,
My lips shall praise You.
Thus I will bless You while I live;
I will lift up my hands in Your name.

PSALM 63:3–4

Oh, give thanks to the LORD, for He is good!
For His mercy endures forever.
Oh, give thanks to the God of gods!
For His mercy endures forever.
Oh, give thanks to the Lord of lords!
For His mercy endures forever:
To Him who alone does great wonders,
For His mercy endures forever.

PSALM 136:1–4

In God (I will praise His word),
In the LORD (I will praise His word).

PSALM 56:10

I will bless the LORD at all times;
His praise shall continually be in my mouth.

PSALM 34:1

Whoever offers praise glorifies Me;
And to him who orders his conduct aright
I will show the salvation of God.

PSALM 50:23

We are hard pressed on every side, yet not crushed; we are perplexed, but not in despair; persecuted, but not forsaken; struck down, but not destroyed— always carrying about in the body the dying of the Lord Jesus, that the life of Jesus also may be manifested in our body. For we who live are always delivered to death for Jesus' sake, that the life of Jesus also may be manifested in our mortal flesh.

2 CORINTHIANS 4:8–11

For our light affliction, which is but for a moment, is working for us a far more exceeding and eternal weight of glory, while we do not look at the things which are seen, but at the things which are not seen. For the things which are seen are temporary, but the things which are not seen are eternal.

2 CORINTHIANS 4:17–18

Therefore do not cast away your confidence, which has great reward. For you have need of endurance, so that after you have done the will of God, you may receive the promise.

HEBREWS 10:35–36

*God's Promises*

Through the LORD's mercies we are not
consumed,
Because His compassions fail not.
They are new every morning;
Great is Your faithfulness.
"The LORD is my portion," says my soul,
"Therefore I hope in Him!"
The LORD is good to those who wait for Him,
To the soul who seeks Him.

LAMENTATIONS 3:22–25

For we know that if our earthly house, this tent, is
destroyed, we have a building from God, a house not
made with hands, eternal in the heavens.

2 CORINTHIANS 5:1

I would have lost heart, unless I had believed
That I would see the goodness of the LORD
In the land of the living.
Wait on the LORD;
Be of good courage,
And He shall strengthen your heart;
Wait, I say, on the LORD!

PSALM 27:13–14

This hope we have as an anchor of the soul, both sure and steadfast, and which enters the Presence behind the veil.

HEBREWS 6:19

> I wait for the LORD, my soul waits,
> And in His word I do hope.
> My soul waits for the Lord
> More than those who watch for the morning—
> Yes, more than those who watch for
>     the morning.

PSALM 130:5–6

Every morning He brings His justice to light; He never fails.

ZEPHANIAH 3:5

Let us hold fast the confession of our hope without wavering, for He who promised is faithful.

HEBREWS 10:23

# GOD BLESSES WOMEN WHEN THEY . . . REST IN HIS PEACE

For in the time of trouble
He shall hide me in His pavilion;
In the secret place of His tabernacle
He shall hide me;
He shall set me high upon a rock.

PSALM 27:5

Give us help from trouble,
For the help of man is useless.
Through God we will do valiantly,
For it is He who shall tread down our enemies.

PSALM 60:11–12

All your children shall be taught by
    the LORD,
And great shall be the peace of your children.
In righteousness you shall be established;
You shall be far from oppression, for
    you shall not fear;
And from terror, for it shall not come
    near you.

ISAIAH 54:13–14

103

Come to Me, all you who labor . . . and I will give
you rest.

MATTHEW 11:28

The LORD will guide you continually,
And satisfy your soul in drought,
And strengthen your bones;
You shall be like a watered garden,
And like a spring of water, whose waters
    do not fail.

ISAIAH 58:11

The Spirit of the LORD God is upon Me,
Because the LORD has anointed Me
To preach good tidings to the poor;
He has sent Me to heal the brokenhearted,
To proclaim liberty to the captives,
And the opening of the prison to those
    who are bound.

ISAIAH 61:1

Let, I pray, Your merciful kindness be for
    my comfort,
According to Your word to Your servant.
Let Your tender mercies come to me, that
    I may live;
For Your law is my delight.

PSALM 119:76–77

When my father and my mother forsake me,
Then the LORD will take care of me.
I would have lost heart, unless I had believed
That I would see the goodness of the LORD
In the land of the living.
Wait on the LORD;
Be of good courage,
And He shall strengthen your heart;
Wait, I say, on the LORD!

PSALM 27:10, 13, 14

Let the words of my mouth and the
      meditation of my heart
Be acceptable in Your sight,
O LORD, my strength and my Redeemer.

PSALM 19:14

Anxiety in the heart . . . causes depression, but a good
word makes it glad.

PROVERBS 12:25

You, beloved, building yourselves up on your most holy faith, praying in the Holy Spirit, keep yourselves in the love of God, looking for the mercy of our Lord Jesus Christ unto eternal life.

JUDE 20–21

Be anxious for nothing, but in everything by prayer and supplication, with thanksgiving, let your requests be made known to God; and the peace of God, which surpasses all understanding, will guard your hearts and minds through Christ Jesus.

PHILIPPIANS 4:6–7

Therefore, having been justified by faith, we have peace with God through our Lord Jesus Christ, through whom also we have access by faith into this grace in which we stand, and rejoice in hope of the glory of God.

ROMANS 5:1–2

The Lord is faithful, who will establish you and guard you from the evil one.

2 THESSALONIANS 3:3

My soul, wait silently for God alone,
For my expectation is from Him.
He only is my rock and my salvation;
He is my defense;
I shall not be moved.
In God is my salvation and my glory;
The rock of my strength,
And my refuge, is in God.

PSALM 62:5–7

Without faith it is impossible to please Him, for he who comes to God must believe that He is, and that He is a rewarder of those who diligently seek Him.

HEBREWS 11:6

As Moses lifted up the serpent in the wilderness, even so must the Son of Man be lifted up, that whoever believes in Him should not perish but have eternal life.

JOHN 3:14–15

Now faith is the substance of things hoped for, the evidence of things not seen. For by it the elders obtained a good testimony.

By faith we understand that the worlds were framed by the word of God, so that the things which are seen were not made of things which are visible.

HEBREWS 11:1–3

He has put a new song in my mouth—
Praise to our God;
Many will see it and fear,
And will trust in the LORD.

PSALM 40:3

The Spirit Himself bears witness with our spirit that we are children of God, and if children, then heirs—heirs of God and joint heirs with Christ, if indeed we suffer with Him, that we may also be glorified together.

For I consider that the sufferings of this present time are not worthy to be compared with the glory which shall be revealed in us.

ROMANS 8:16–18

All that the Father gives Me will come to Me, and the one who comes to Me I will by no means cast out.

JOHN 6:37

Great is the LORD, and greatly to be praised
In the city of our God,
In His holy mountain.

PSALM 48:1

The earth is the LORD's, and all its fullness,
The world and those who dwell therein.
For He has founded it upon the seas,
And established it upon the waters.
Who may ascend into the hill of the LORD?
Or who may stand in His holy place?
He who has clean hands and a pure heart,
Who has not lifted up his soul to an idol,
Nor sworn deceitfully.
He shall receive blessing from the LORD,
And righteousness from the God of his salvation.
This is Jacob, the generation of those
 who seek Him,
Who seek Your face.
Lift up your heads, O you gates!
And be lifted up, you everlasting doors!
And the King of glory shall come in.
Who is this King of glory?
The LORD strong and mighty,
The LORD mighty in battle.
Lift up your heads, O you gates!
Lift up, you everlasting doors!
And the King of glory shall come in.
Who is this King of glory?
The LORD of hosts,
He is the King of glory.

PSALM 24:1–10

*God's Promises*

The LORD is near to those who have a
    broken heart,
And saves such as have a contrite spirit.
Many are the afflictions of the righteous,
But the LORD delivers him out of them all.

PSALM 34:18–19

The LORD is your keeper;
The LORD is your shade at your right hand.
The sun shall not strike you by day,
Nor the moon by night.
The LORD shall preserve you from all evil;
He shall preserve your soul.
The LORD shall preserve your going out
    and your coming in
From this time forth, and even forevermore.

PSALM 121:5–8

For God is the King of all the earth;
Sing praises with understanding.
God reigns over the nations;
God sits on His holy throne.
The princes of the people have gathered
        together,
The people of the God of Abraham.
For the shields of the earth belong to God;
He is greatly exalted.

PSALM 47:7–9

GOD COMFORTS
WOMEN AS THEY
LEARN TO . . .

Beloved, do not forget this one thing, that with the Lord one day is as a thousand years, and a thousand years as one day. The Lord is not slack concerning His promise, as some count slackness, but is longsuffering toward us, not willing that any should perish but that all should come to repentance.

2 PETER 3:8–9

Cast your burden on the LORD,
And He shall sustain you;
He shall never permit the righteous to
        be moved.

PSALM 55:22

Blessed is the man who endures temptation; for when he has been approved, he will receive the crown of life which the Lord has promised to those who love Him.

For if anyone is a hearer of the word and not a doer, he is like a man observing his natural face in a mirror; for he observes himself, goes away, and immediately forgets what kind of man he was.

JAMES 1:12, 23–24

But He knows the way that I take;
When He has tested me, I shall come forth
    as gold.
My foot has held fast to His steps;
I have kept His way and not turned aside.

JOB 23:10–11

Why are you cast down, O my soul?
And why are you disquieted within me?
Hope in God;
For I shall yet praise Him,
The help of my countenance and my God.

PSALM 43:5

Beloved, do not think it strange concerning the fiery trial which is to try you, as though some strange thing happened to you; but rejoice to the extent that you partake of Christ's sufferings, that when His glory is revealed, you may also be glad with exceeding joy.

Yet if anyone suffers as a Christian, let him not be ashamed, but let him glorify God in this matter.

1 PETER 4:12–13, 16

I command you today to love the LORD your God, to walk in His ways, and to keep His commandments.

DEUTERONOMY 30:16

Hear me, O LORD, for Your lovingkindness
    is good;
Turn to me according to the multitude of
      Your tender mercies.
And do not hide Your face from Your servant,
For I am in trouble;
Hear me speedily.
Draw near to my soul, and redeem it;
Deliver me because of my enemies.

PSALM 69:16–18

He who covers his sins will not prosper,
But whoever confesses and forsakes them
    will have mercy.

PROVERBS 28:13

Blessed are those who keep His testimonies, who seek
Him with the whole heart.

PSALM 119:2

Be ye doers of the word, and not hearers only, deceiving
yourselves.

JAMES 1:22

Heal me, O LORD, and I shall be healed;
Save me, and I shall be saved,
For You are my praise.

JEREMIAH 17:14


I said, "This is my anguish;
But I will remember the years of the
          right hand of the Most High."
I will remember the works of the LORD;
Surely I will remember Your wonders of old.
I will also meditate on all Your work,
And talk of Your deeds.
Your way, O God, is in the sanctuary;
Who is so great a God as our God?
You are the God who does wonders;
You have declared Your strength among
          the peoples.

PSALM 77:10–14


For this is God,
Our God forever and ever;
He will be our guide
Even to death.

PSALM 48:14

God will redeem my soul from the power
     of the grave,
For He shall receive me.

PSALM 49:15

Yea, though I walk through the valley of the
     shadow of death,
I will fear no evil;
For You are with me;
Your rod and Your staff, they comfort me.

PSALM 23:4

For we know that if our earthly house, this tent, is
destroyed, we have a building from God, a house not
made with hands, eternal in the heavens.

2 CORINTHIANS 5:1

While I live I will praise the LORD;
I will sing praises to my God while I have my
     being.

PSALM 146:2

Before I was afflicted I went astray,
But now I keep Your word.
You are good, and do good;
Teach me Your statutes.

PSALM 119:67–68

The Lord said, "Who then is that faithful and wise steward, whom his master will make ruler over his household, to give them their portion of food in due season? Blessed is that servant whom his master will find so doing when he comes. Truly, I say to you that he will make him ruler over all that he has."

LUKE 12:42–44

Pray for the peace of Jerusalem:
May they prosper who love you.

PSALM 122:6

When He had fasted forty days and forty nights, afterward He was hungry. Now when the tempter came to Him, he said, "If You are the Son of God, command that these stones become bread."

But He answered and said, "It is written, 'Man shall not live by bread alone, but by every word that proceeds from the mouth of God.'"

MATTHEW 4:2–4

My God shall supply all your need according to His riches in glory by Christ Jesus.

PHILIPPIANS 4:19

Listen, my beloved brethren: Has God not chosen the poor of this world to be rich in faith and heirs of the kingdom which He promised to those who love Him?

JAMES 2:5

He who trusts in his riches will fall,
But the righteous will flourish like foliage.

PROVERBS 11:28

Then He said to His disciples, "Therefore I say to you, do not worry about your life, what you will eat; nor about the body, what you will put on. Life is more than food, and the body is more than clothing. Consider the ravens, for they neither sow nor reap, which have neither storehouse nor barn; and God feeds them. Of how much more value are you than the birds?"

LUKE 12:22–24

Poverty and shame will come to him who
disdains correction,
But he who regards a rebuke will be honored.

PROVERBS 13:18

For now we see in a mirror, dimly, but then face to face. Now I know in part, but then I shall know just as I also am known.

1 CORINTHIANS 13:12

> The righteous shall flourish like a palm tree,
> He shall grow like a cedar in Lebanon.
> Those who are planted in the house of the
>     LORD
> Shall flourish in the courts of our God.
> They shall still bear fruit in old age;
> They shall be fresh and flourishing,
> To declare that the LORD is upright;
> He is my rock, and there is no
>         unrighteousness in Him.

PSALM 92:12–15

For none of us lives to himself, and no one dies to himself. For if we live, we live to the Lord; and if we die, we die to the Lord. Therefore, whether we live or die, we are the Lord's.

ROMANS 14:7–8

The fear of the LORD prolongs days,
But the years of the wicked will be shortened.
PROVERBS 10:27


The days of our lives are seventy years;
And if by reason of strength they are
eighty years,
Yet their boast is only labor and sorrow;
For it is soon cut off, and we fly away.
So teach us to number our days,
That we may gain a heart of wisdom.
Oh, satisfy us early with Your mercy,
That we may rejoice and be glad all our days!
PSALM 90:10, 12, 14


Older men be sober, reverent, temperate, sound in faith, in love, in patience; the older women likewise, that they be reverent in behavior, not slanderers, not given to much wine, teachers of good things— that they admonish the young women to love their husbands, to love their children.

TITUS 2:2–4

But as for me, I trust in You, O LORD;
I say, "You are my God."
My times are in Your hand;
Deliver me from the hand of my enemies,
And from those who persecute me.

PSALM 31:14–15


For I know that my Redeemer lives,
And He shall stand at last on the earth;
And after my skin is destroyed, this I know,
That in my flesh I shall see God.

JOB 19:25–26

I will both lie down in peace, and sleep;
For You alone, O LORD, make me dwell
    in safety.

PSALM 4:8

The angel of the LORD encamps all around
    those who fear Him,
And delivers them.

PSALM 34:7

He who dwells in the secret place of the
    Most High
Shall abide under the shadow of the Almighty.
I will say of the LORD, "He is my refuge and
    my fortress;
My God, in Him I will trust."

PSALM 91:1–2

Are not two sparrows sold for a copper coin? And not
one of them falls to the ground apart from your
Father's will. But the very hairs of your head are all
numbered. Do not fear therefore; you are of more
value than many sparrows.

MATTHEW 10:29–31

So shall they fear
The name of the LORD from the west,
And His glory from the rising of the sun;
When the enemy comes in like a flood,
The Spirit of the LORD will lift up a standard
      against him.

ISAIAH 59:19

The LORD is my light and my salvation;
Whom shall I fear?
The LORD is the strength of my life;
Of whom shall I be afraid?
For in the time of trouble
He shall hide me in His pavilion;
In the secret place of His tabernacle
He shall hide me;
He shall set me high upon a rock.

PSALM 27:1, 5

The eternal God is your refuge,
And underneath are the everlasting arms;
He will thrust out the enemy from before you,
And will say, "Destroy!"

DEUTERONOMY 33:27

Whoever listens to me will dwell safely,
And will be secure, without fear of evil.

PROVERBS 1:33

"For the mountains shall depart
  And the hills be removed,
  But My kindness shall not depart from you,
  Nor shall My covenant of peace be removed,"
  Says the LORD, who has mercy on you.
"All your children shall be taught by the
      LORD,
  And great shall be the peace of your children.
  No weapon formed against you shall prosper,
  And every tongue which rises against you in
      judgment
  You shall condemn.
  This is the heritage of the servants of the LORD,
  And their righteousness is from Me,"
  Says the LORD.

ISAIAH 54:10, 13, 17

Not that I speak in regard to need, for I have learned
in whatever state I am, to be content: I know how to
be abased, and I know how to abound. Everywhere
and in all things I have learned both to be full and to
be hungry, both to abound and to suffer need.

PHILIPPIANS 4:11–12

There is therefore now no condemnation to those who are in Christ Jesus, who do not walk according to the flesh, but according to the Spirit. For the law of the Spirit of life in Christ Jesus has made me free from the law of sin and death.

For those who live according to the flesh set their minds on the things of the flesh, but those who live according to the Spirit, the things of the Spirit. For to be carnally minded is death, but to be spiritually minded is life and peace.

ROMANS 8:1–2, 5–6

Now godliness with contentment is great gain. For we brought nothing into this world, and it is certain we can carry nothing out. And having food and clothing, with these we shall be content.

1 TIMOTHY 6:6–8

The LORD is my shepherd;
I shall not want.

PSALM 23:1

Not that we are sufficient of ourselves to think of anything as being from ourselves, but our sufficiency is from God.

2 CORINTHIANS 3:5

The LORD will guide you continually,
And satisfy your soul in drought,
And strengthen your bones;
You shall be like a watered garden,
And like a spring of water, whose waters
    do not fail.

ISAIAH 58:11

The LORD is your keeper;
The LORD is your shade at your right hand.
The LORD shall preserve your going out
    and your coming in
From this time forth, and even forevermore.

PSALM 121:5, 8

Eye has not seen, nor ear heard . . . the things which
God has prepared for those who love Him.

1 CORINTHIANS 2:9

You are complete in Him, who is the head of all principality and power.

COLOSSIANS 2:10

GOD GIVES FREELY
TO WOMEN . . .

# GOD GIVES FREELY TO WOMEN . . . HOPE FOR ETERNAL LIFE

Sing to the LORD with thanksgiving;
Sing praises on the harp to our God,
Who covers the heavens with clouds,
Who prepares rain for the earth,
Who makes grass to grow on the mountains.
He gives to the beast its food,
And to the young ravens that cry.
He does not delight in the strength of the
    horse;
He takes no pleasure in the legs of a man.
The LORD takes pleasure in those who fear
    Him,
In those who hope in His mercy.
Praise the LORD, O Jerusalem!
Praise your God, O Zion!
For He has strengthened the bars of your
    gates;
He has blessed your children within you.

PSALM 147:7–13

If then you were raised with Christ, seek those things which are above, where Christ is, sitting at the right hand of God. Set your mind on things above, not on things on the earth. For you died, and your life is hidden with Christ in God. When Christ who is our life appears, then you also will appear with Him in glory.

COLOSSIANS 3:1–4

Let us who are of the day be sober, putting on the breastplate of faith and love, and as a helmet the hope of salvation. For God did not appoint us to wrath, but to obtain salvation through our Lord Jesus Christ, who died for us, that whether we wake or sleep, we should live   together with Him.

Therefore comfort each other and edify one another, just as you also are doing.

1 THESSALONIANS 5:8–11

God, who is rich in mercy, because of His great love with which He loved us, even when we were dead in trespasses, made us alive together with Christ (by grace you have been saved), and raised us up together, and made us sit together in the heavenly places in Christ Jesus, that in the ages to come He might show the exceeding riches of His grace in His kindness toward us in Christ Jesus.

EPHESIANS 2:4–7

Knowing that a man is not justified by the works of the law but by faith in Jesus Christ, even we have believed in Christ Jesus, that we might be justified by faith in Christ and not by the works of the law; for by the works of the law no flesh shall be justified.

I have been crucified with Christ; it is no longer I who live, but Christ lives in me; and the life which I now live in the flesh I live by faith in the Son of God, who loved me and gave Himself for me.

GALATIANS 2:16, 20

For as many as are led by the Spirit of God, these are sons of God. For you did not receive the spirit of bondage again to fear, but you received the Spirit of adoption by whom we cry out, "Abba, Father." The Spirit Himself bears witness with our spirit that we are children of God, and if children, then heirs—heirs of God and joint heirs with Christ, if indeed we suffer with Him, that we may also be glorified together.

For I consider that the sufferings of this present time are not worthy to be compared with the glory which shall be revealed in us.

For we were saved in this hope, but hope that is seen is not hope; for why does one still hope for what he sees? But if we hope for what we do not see, we eagerly wait for it with perseverance.

ROMANS 8:14–18, 24–25

I have fought the good fight, I have finished the race, I have kept the faith. Finally, there is laid up for me the crown of righteousness, which the Lord, the righteous Judge, will give to me on that Day, and not to me only but also to all who have loved His appearing.

2 TIMOTHY 4:7–8

Blessed be the God and Father of our Lord Jesus Christ, who according to His abundant mercy has begotten us again to a living hope through the resurrection of Jesus Christ from the dead, to an inheritance incorruptible and undefiled and that does not fade away, reserved in heaven for you, who are kept by the power of God through faith for salvation ready to be revealed in the last time.

In this you greatly rejoice, though now for a little while, if need be, you have been grieved by various trials, that the genuineness of your faith, being much more precious than gold that perishes, though it is tested by fire, may be found to praise, honor, and glory at the revelation of Jesus Christ, whom having not seen you love. Though now you do not see Him, yet believing, you rejoice with joy inexpressible and full of glory, receiving the end of your faith—the salvation of your souls.

1 PETER 1:3–9

Because of the hope which is laid up for you in heaven, of which you heard before in the word of the truth of the gospel, which has come to you, as it has also in all the world, and is bringing forth fruit, as it is also among you since the day you heard and knew the grace of God in truth.

Colossians 1:5–6

My son, pay attention to my wisdom;
Lend your ear to my understanding,
That you may preserve discretion,
And your lips may keep knowledge.

PROVERBS 5:1–2

The fear of the LORD is the beginning of
     wisdom;
A good understanding have all those who do
     His commandments.
His praise endures forever.

PSALM 111:10

The days of our lives are seventy years;
And if by reason of strength they are
     eighty years,
Yet their boast is only labor and sorrow;
For it is soon cut off, and we fly away.
Who knows the power of Your anger?
For as the fear of You, so is Your wrath.
So teach us to number our days,
That we may gain a heart of wisdom.

PSALM 90:10–12

*God's Promises*

Happy is the man who finds wisdom,
And the man who gains understanding;
For her proceeds are better than the profits
　　of silver,
And her gain than fine gold.
She is more precious than rubies,
And all the things you may desire cannot
　　compare with her.
Length of days is in her right hand,
In her left hand riches and honor.
Her ways are ways of pleasantness,
And all her paths are peace.
She is a tree of life to those who take hold
　　of her,
And happy are all who retain her.
The LORD by wisdom founded the earth;
By understanding He established the heavens;
By His knowledge the depths were
　　broken up,
And clouds drop down the dew.
My son, let them not depart from
　　your eyes—
Keep sound wisdom and discretion;
So they will be life to your soul
And grace to your neck.

PROVERBS 3:13–22

A wise man fears and departs from evil,
But a fool rages and is self-confident.

PROVERBS 14:16

Get wisdom! Get understanding!
Do not forget, nor turn away from the
    words of my mouth.
Do not forsake her, and she will
    preserve you;
Love her, and she will keep you.
Wisdom is the principal thing;
Therefore get wisdom.
And in all your getting, get understanding.
Exalt her, and she will promote you;
She will bring you honor, when you
    embrace her.
She will place on your head an ornament
    of grace;
A crown of glory she will deliver to you.
Hear, my son, and receive my sayings,
And the years of your life will be many.
I have taught you in the way of wisdom;
I have led you in right paths.

PROVERBS 4:5–11

*God's Promises*

If any of you lacks wisdom, let him ask of God, who gives to all liberally and without reproach, and it will be given to him. But let him ask in faith, with no doubting, for he who doubts is like a wave of the sea driven and tossed by the wind.

JAMES 1:5–6

How much better to get wisdom than gold!
And to get understanding is to be
    chosen rather than silver.

PROVERBS 16:16

My son, keep my words,
And treasure my commands within you.
Keep my commands and live,
And my law as the apple of your eye.
Bind them on your fingers;
Write them on the tablet of your heart.
Say to wisdom, "You are my sister,"
And call understanding your nearest kin,
That they may keep you from the immoral
    woman,
From the seductress who flatters with her
    words.

PROVERBS 7:1–5

The fear of the LORD is the beginning of
     wisdom,
And the knowledge of the Holy One is
     understanding.
For by me your days will be multiplied,
And years of life will be added to you.
If you are wise, you are wise for yourself,
And if you scoff, you will bear it alone.

PROVERBS 9:10–12

The wisdom that is from above is first pure, then
peaceable, gentle, willing to yield, full of mercy and
good fruits, without partiality and without hypocrisy.

JAMES 3:17

Therefore, if anyone is in Christ, he is a new creation; old things have passed away; behold, all things have become new. Now all things are of God, who has reconciled us to Himself through Jesus Christ, and has given us the ministry of reconciliation, that is, that God was in Christ reconciling the world to Himself, not imputing their trespasses to them, and has committed to us the word of reconciliation.

Now then, we are ambassadors for Christ, as though God were pleading through us: we implore you on Christ's behalf, be reconciled to God. For He made Him who knew no sin to be sin for us, that we might become the righteousness of God in Him.

2 CORINTHIANS 5:17–21

O God, You know my foolishness;
And my sins are not hidden from You.

PSALM 69:5

It is no longer I who live, but Christ lives in me.

GALATIANS 2:20

For as many as are of the works of the law are under the curse; for it is written, "Cursed is everyone who does not continue in all things which are written in the book of the law, to do them." But that no one is justified by the law in the sight of God is evident, for the just shall live by faith.

GALATIANS 3:10–11

Stand fast therefore in the liberty by which Christ has made us free, and do not be entangled again with a yoke of bondage.

GALATIANS 5:1

This is the message which we have heard from Him and declare to you, that God is light and in Him is no darkness at all. If we say that we have fellowship with Him, and walk in darkness, we lie and do not practice the truth. But if we walk in the light as He is in the light, we have fellowship with one another, and the blood of Jesus Christ His Son cleanses us from all sin.

If we say that we have no sin, we deceive ourselves, and the truth is not in us. If we confess our sins, He is faithful and just to forgive us our sins and to cleanse us from all unrighteousness. If we say that we have not sinned, we make Him a liar, and His word is not in us.

1 JOHN 1:5–10

Create in me a clean heart, O God, and renew a steadfast spirit within me.

PSALM 51:10

> "Wash yourselves, make yourselves clean;
>      Put away the evil of your doings from
>            before My eyes.
>      Cease to do evil,
>      Learn to do good;
>      Seek justice,
>      Rebuke the oppressor;
>      Defend the fatherless,
>      Plead for the widow.
>      Come now, and let us reason together,"
>      Says the LORD,
> "Though your sins are like scarlet,
>      They shall be as white as snow;
>      Though they are red like crimson,
>      They shall be as wool.
>      If you are willing and obedient,
>      You shall eat the good of the land."

ISAIAH 1:16–19

I have taught you in the way of wisdom; I have led
you in right paths.

PROVERBS 4:11

You know that He was manifested to take away our sins, and in Him there is no sin. Whoever abides in Him does not sin. Whoever sins has neither seen Him nor known Him. Little children, let no one deceive you. He who practices righteousness is righteous, just as He is righteous.

1 JOHN 3:5–7

Therefore, since we have this ministry, as we have received mercy, we do not lose heart. But we have renounced the hidden things of shame, not walking in craftiness nor handling the word of God deceitfully, but by manifestation of the truth commending ourselves to every man's conscience in the sight of God. But even if our gospel is veiled, it is veiled to those who are perishing, whose minds the god of this age has blinded, who do not believe, lest the light of the gospel of the glory of Christ, who is the image of God, should shine on them. For we do not preach ourselves, but Christ Jesus the Lord, and ourselves your bondservants for Jesus' sake. For it is the God who commanded light to shine out of darkness, who has shone in our hearts to give the light of the knowledge of the glory of God in the face of Jesus Christ.

2 CORINTHIANS 4:1–6

The LORD builds up Jerusalem;
He gathers together the outcasts of Israel.
He heals the brokenhearted
And binds up their wounds.
Great is our Lord, and mighty in power;
His understanding is infinite.
The LORD lifts up the humble;
He casts the wicked down to the ground.
For He has strengthened the bars of your
          gates;
He has blessed your children within you.
He makes peace in your borders,
And fills you with the finest wheat.

PSALM 147:2–3, 5–6, 13–14

Peace I leave with you, My peace I give to you; not as the world gives do I give to you. Let not your heart be troubled, neither let it be afraid.

JOHN 14:27

Turn Yourself to me, and have mercy on me,
For I am desolate and afflicted.
The troubles of my heart have enlarged;
Bring me out of my distresses!
Look on my affliction and my pain,
And forgive all my sins.

PSALM 25:16–18

Casting all your care upon Him, for He cares for you.
Be sober, be vigilant; because your adversary the devil walks about like a roaring lion, seeking whom he may devour. Resist him, steadfast in the faith, knowing that the same sufferings are experienced by your brotherhood in the world. But may the God of all grace, who called us to His eternal glory by Christ Jesus, after you have suffered a while, perfect, establish, strengthen, and settle you. To Him be the glory and the dominion forever and ever. Amen.

1 PETER 5:7–11

I will be glad and rejoice in Your mercy,
For You have considered my trouble;
You have known my soul in adversities.

PSALM 31:7

A horse is a vain hope for safety;
Neither shall it deliver any by its
    great strength.
Behold, the eye of the LORD is on those
    who fear Him,
On those who hope in His mercy,
To deliver their soul from death,
And to keep them alive in famine.
Our soul waits for the LORD;
He is our help and our shield.
For our heart shall rejoice in Him,
Because we have trusted in His holy name.
Let Your mercy, O LORD, be upon us,
Just as we hope in You.

                      PSALM 33:17–22

For none of us lives to himself, and no one dies to himself.

                      ROMANS 14:7

I will bless the LORD at all times;
His praise shall continually be in my mouth.
My soul shall make its boast in the LORD;
The humble shall hear of it and be glad.
Oh, magnify the LORD with me,
And let us exalt His name together.
I sought the LORD, and He heard me,
And delivered me from all my fears.
They looked to Him and were radiant,
And their faces were not ashamed.
This poor man cried out, and the
      LORD heard him,
And saved him out of all his troubles.
The angel of the LORD encamps all
      around those who fear Him,
And delivers them.
Oh, taste and see that the LORD is good;
Blessed is the man who trusts in Him!

PSALM 34:1–8

Yet in all these things we are more than conquerors
through Him who loved us. For I am persuaded that
neither death nor life, nor angels nor principalities
nor powers, nor things present nor things to come,
nor height nor depth, nor any other created thing,
shall be able to separate us from the love of God
which is in Christ Jesus our Lord.

ROMANS 8:37–39

For You will light my lamp;
The LORD my God will enlighten my
    darkness.
For by You I can run against a troop,
By my God I can leap over a wall.
As for God, His way is perfect;
The word of the LORD is proven;
He is a shield to all who trust in Him.

PSALM 18:28–30

The LORD is my light and my salvation;
Whom shall I fear?
The LORD is the strength of my life;
Of whom shall I be afraid?

When the wicked came against me
To eat up my flesh,
My enemies and foes,
They stumbled and fell.
Though an army may encamp against me,
My heart shall not fear;
Though war may rise against me,
In this I will be confident.
One thing I have desired of the LORD,
That will I seek:
That I may dwell in the house of the LORD
All the days of my life,
To behold the beauty of the LORD,
And to inquire in His temple.
For in the time of trouble
He shall hide me in His pavilion;
In the secret place of His tabernacle
He shall hide me;
He shall set me high upon a rock.
And now my head shall be lifted up above
      my enemies all around me;
Therefore I will offer sacrifices of joy in His
      tabernacle;
I will sing, yes, I will sing praises to the LORD.
Hear, O LORD, when I cry with my voice!
Have mercy also upon me, and answer me.

PSALM 27:1–7

Do not be afraid of sudden terror,
Nor of trouble from the wicked when
    it comes;
For the LORD will be your confidence,
And will keep your foot from being caught.

PROVERBS 3:25–26

The LORD your God himself crosses over before you
. . . He will be with you, He will not leave you nor
forsake you.

DEUTERONOMY 31:3, 8

Your ears shall hear a voice behind you saying, "This
is the way; walk in it."

ISAIAH 30:21

Let us therefore come boldly to the throne of grace,
that we may obtain mercy and find grace to help in
time of need.

HEBREWS 4:16

Then Jesus spoke to them again, saying, "I am the
light of the world. He who follows Me shall not walk
in darkness, but have the light of life."

JOHN 8:12

Delight yourself also in the LORD,
And He shall give you the desires of your
heart.
Commit your way to the LORD,
Trust also in Him,
And He shall bring it to pass.
He shall bring forth your righteousness
as the light,
And your justice as the noonday.

PSALM 37:4–6


I will love You, O LORD, my strength.
The LORD is my rock and my fortress and
my deliverer;
My God, my strength, in whom I will trust;
My shield and the horn of my salvation, my
stronghold.
I will call upon the LORD, who is worthy to
be praised;
So shall I be saved from my enemies.

PSALM 18:1–3

Blessed is the man
Who walks not in the counsel of the ungodly,
Nor stands in the path of sinners,
Nor sits in the seat of the scornful;
But his delight is in the law of the LORD,
And in His law he meditates day and night.
He shall be like a tree
Planted by the rivers of water,
That brings forth its fruit in its season,
Whose leaf also shall not wither;
And whatever he does shall prosper.
The ungodly are not so,
But are like the chaff which the wind drives
　　　away.
Therefore the ungodly shall not stand in
　　　the judgment,
Nor sinners in the congregation of the righteous.
For the LORD knows the way of the
　　　righteous,
But the way of the ungodly shall perish.

PSALM 1:1–6

The LORD shall judge the peoples;
Judge me, O LORD, according to my
    righteousness,
And according to my integrity within me.

PSALM 7:8

The righteous man walks in his integrity;
His children are blessed after him.

PROVERBS 20:7

He who speaks truth declares righteousness,
But a false witness, deceit.
There is one who speaks like the piercings
    of a sword,
But the tongue of the wise promotes health.
The truthful lip shall be established forever,
But a lying tongue is but for a moment.

PROVERBS 12:17–19

A good man deals graciously and lends;
He will guide his affairs with discretion.
Surely he will never be shaken;
The righteous will be in everlasting
    remembrance.
He will not be afraid of evil tidings;
His heart is steadfast, trusting in the LORD.

PSALM 112:5–7

I will behave wisely in a perfect way.
Oh, when will You come to me?
I will walk within my house with a
      perfect heart.
I will set nothing wicked before my eyes;
I hate the work of those who fall away;
It shall not cling to me.
A perverse heart shall depart from me;
I will not know wickedness.
Whoever secretly slanders his neighbor,
Him I will destroy;
The one who has a haughty look and a
      proud heart,
Him I will not endure.
My eyes shall be on the faithful of the land,
That they may dwell with me;
He who walks in a perfect way,
He shall serve me.
He who works deceit shall not dwell within
      my house;
He who tells lies shall not continue in my
      presence.
Early I will destroy all the wicked of the land,
That I may cut off all the evildoers from the
      city of the LORD.

PSALM 101:2–8

*God's Promises*

The LORD shall judge the peoples;
Judge me, O LORD, according to my
    righteousness,
And according to my integrity within me.

PSALM 7:8

If I have walked with falsehood,
Or if my foot has hastened to deceit,
Let me be weighed on honest scales,
That God may know my integrity.

JOB 31:5–6

Far be it from me
That I should say you are right;
Till I die I will not put away my integrity
    from me.
My righteousness I hold fast, and will not let
    it go;
My heart shall not reproach me as long as
    I live.

JOB 27:5–6

Blessed are the undefiled in the way,
Who walk in the law of the LORD!
Blessed are those who keep His testimonies,
Who seek Him with the whole heart!
They also do no iniquity;
They walk in His ways.
You have commanded us
To keep Your precepts diligently.
Oh, that my ways were directed
To keep Your statutes!
Then I would not be ashamed,
When I look into all Your commandments.
I will praise You with uprightness of heart,
When I learn Your righteous judgments.
I will keep Your statutes;
Oh, do not forsake me utterly!

PSALM 119:1–8

# GOD HELPS WOMEN TO GROW BY . . .

There is a way that seems right to a man,
But its end is the way of death.

PROVERBS 14:12

Beware of false prophets, who come to you in sheep's clothing, but inwardly they are ravenous wolves. You will know them by their fruits. Do men gather grapes from thornbushes or figs from thistles?

MATTHEW 7:15–16

By this you know the Spirit of God: Every spirit that confesses that Jesus Christ has come in the flesh is of God, and every spirit that does not confess that Jesus Christ has come in the flesh is not of God. And this is the spirit of the Antichrist, which you have heard was coming, and is now already in the world.

1 JOHN 4:2–3

For God is not the author of confusion but of peace, as in all the churches of the saints.

1 CORINTHIANS 14:33

They profess to know God, but in works they deny Him, being abominable, disobedient, and disqualified for every good work.

TITUS 1:16

For God has not given us a spirit of fear, but of power and of love and of a sound mind.

2 TIMOTHY 1:7

For certain men have crept in unnoticed, who long ago were marked out for this condemnation, ungodly men, who turn the grace of our God into lewdness and deny the only Lord God and our Lord Jesus Christ.

JUDE 4

For many deceivers have gone out into the world who do not confess Jesus Christ as coming in the flesh. This is a deceiver and an antichrist.

Whoever transgresses and does not abide in the doctrine of Christ does not have God. He who abides in the doctrine of Christ has both the Father and the Son. If anyone comes to you and does not bring this doctrine, do not receive him into your house nor greet him; for he who greets him shares in his evil deeds.

2 JOHN 7, 9–11

Your word is a lamp to my feet and a light to my path.

PSALM 119:105

Let no corrupt word proceed out of your mouth, but
what is good for necessary edification, that it may
impart grace to the hearers.

EPHESIANS 4:29

As long as my breath is in me,
And the breath of God in my nostrils,
My lips will not speak wickedness,
Nor my tongue utter deceit.

JOB 27:3–4

He who would love life
And see good days,
Let him refrain his tongue from evil,
And his lips from speaking deceit.

1 PETER 3:10

Do not be a witness against your
        neighbor without cause,
For would you deceive with your lips?

PROVERBS 24:28

Whoever guards his mouth and tongue
Keeps his soul from troubles.

PROVERBS 21:23

A good man out of the good treasure of his heart
brings forth good; and an evil man out of the evil
treasure of his heart brings forth evil. For out of the
abundance of the heart his mouth speaks.

LUKE 6:45

A wholesome tongue is a tree of life,
But perverseness in it breaks the spirit.

PROVERBS 15:4

If anyone among you thinks he is religious, and does
not bridle his tongue but deceives his own heart, this
one's religion is useless.

JAMES 1:26

Whoever offers praise glorifies Me;
And to him who orders his conduct aright
I will show the salvation of God.

PSALM 50:23

Set a guard, O LORD, over my mouth;
Keep watch over the door of my lips.

PSALM 141:3

Submit to God. Resist the devil and he will flee from you.

JAMES 4:7

I say then: Walk in the Spirit, and you shall not fulfill the lust of the flesh. For the flesh lusts against the Spirit, and the Spirit against the flesh; and these are contrary to one another, so that you do not do the things that you wish.

GALATIANS 5:16–17

Each one is tempted when he is drawn away by his own desires and enticed. Then, when desire has conceived, it gives birth to sin; and sin, when it is full-grown, brings forth death.

Do not be deceived, my beloved brethren.

JAMES 1:14–16

Then the Lord knows how to deliver the godly out of temptations and to reserve the unjust under punishment for the day of judgment.

2 PETER 2:9

A man with an evil eye hastens after riches,
And does not consider that poverty
    will come upon him.

PROVERBS 28:22

For this you know, that no fornicator, unclean person, nor covetous man, who is an idolater, has any inheritance in the kingdom of Christ and God.

Therefore do not be partakers with them.

For you were once darkness, but now you are light in the Lord. Walk as children of light (for the fruit of the Spirit is in all goodness, righteousness, and truth).

And do not be drunk with wine, in which is dissipation; but be filled with the Spirit.

EPHESIANS 5:5, 7–9, 18

That you put off, concerning your former conduct, the old man which grows corrupt according to the deceitful lusts, and be renewed in the spirit of your mind, and that you put on the new man which was created according to God, in true righteousness and holiness.

Nor give place to the devil.

EPHESIANS 4:22–24, 27

*God's Promises*

The LORD is far from the wicked,
But He hears the prayer of the righteous.
PROVERBS 15:29

Likewise you also, reckon yourselves to be dead indeed to sin, but alive to God in Christ Jesus our Lord.

Therefore do not let sin reign in your mortal body, that you should obey it in its lusts.
ROMANS 6:11–12

Do not be conformed to this world, but be transformed by the renewing of your mind, that you may prove what is that good and acceptable and perfect will of God.

ROMANS 12:2

Have no fellowship with the unfruitful works of darkness, but rather expose them.

EPHESIANS 5:11

Then He said to them all, "If anyone desires to come after Me, let him deny himself, and take up his cross daily, and follow Me. For whoever desires to save his life will lose it, but whoever loses his life for My sake will save it. For what profit is it to a man if he gains the whole world, and is himself destroyed or lost?"

LUKE 9:23–25

He said to them, "Take heed and beware of covetousness, for one's life does not consist in the abundance of the things he possesses."

LUKE 12:15

Do not love the world or the things in the world. If anyone loves the world, the love of the Father is not in him. For all that is in the world—the lust of the flesh, the lust of the eyes, and the pride of life—is not of the Father but is of the world. And the world is passing away, and the lust of it; but he who does the will of God abides forever.

1 JOHN 2:15–17

We have renounced the hidden things of shame, not walking in craftiness nor handling the word of God deceitfully, but by manifestation of the truth commending ourselves to every man's conscience in the sight of God.

2 CORINTHIANS 4:2

Set your mind on things above, not on things on the earth.

Do not lie to one another, since you have put off the old man with his deeds, and have put on the new man who is renewed in knowledge according to the image of Him who created him.

COLOSSIANS 3:2, 9–10

Teaching us that, denying ungodliness and worldly lusts, we should live soberly, righteously, and godly in the present age, looking for the blessed hope and glorious appearing of our great God and Savior Jesus Christ.

TITUS 2:12–13

These things I have spoken to you, that in Me you may have peace. In the world you will have tribulation; but be of good cheer, I have overcome the world.

JOHN 16:33

Do not be unequally yoked together with unbelievers. For what fellowship has righteousness with lawlessness? And what communion has light with darkness?

"Come out from among them
And be separate, says the Lord.
Do not touch what is unclean,
And I will receive you."

2 CORINTHIANS 6:14, 17

But you are a chosen generation, a royal priesthood, a holy nation, His own special people.

1 PETER 2:9

Yet it shall not be so among you; but whoever desires to become great among you, let him be your servant. And whoever desires to be first among you, let him be your slave.

MATTHEW 20:26–27

Likewise you younger people, submit yourselves to your elders. Yes, all of you be submissive to one another, and be clothed with humility, for
"God resists the proud,
But gives grace to the humble."
Therefore humble yourselves under the mighty hand of God, that He may exalt you in due time.

1 PETER 5:5–6

A man's pride will bring him low,
But the humble in spirit will retain honor.

PROVERBS 29:23

By humility and the fear of the LORD
Are riches and honor and life.

PROVERBS 22:4

Though the LORD is on high,
Yet He regards the lowly;
But the proud He knows from afar.

PSALM 138:6

The Pharisee stood and prayed thus with himself, "God, I thank You that I am not like other men—extortioners, unjust, adulterers, or even as this tax collector. I fast twice a week; I give tithes of all that I possess." And the tax collector, standing afar off, would not so much as raise his eyes to heaven, but beat his breast, saying, "God, be merciful to me a sinner!" I tell you, this man went down to his house justified rather than the other; for everyone who exalts himself will be humbled, and he who humbles himself will be exalted.

LUKE 18:11–14

He who glories, let him glory in the LORD. For not he who commends himself is approved, but whom the Lord commends.

2 CORINTHIANS 10:17–18

As the elect of God, holy and beloved, put on tender mercies, kindness, humility, meekness, longsuffering.

COLOSSIANS 3:12

Pride goes before destruction,
And a haughty spirit before a fall.
Better to be of a humble spirit with the lowly,
Than to divide the spoil with the proud.
He who heeds the word wisely will
    find good,
And whoever trusts in the LORD, happy is he.

PROVERBS 16:18–20

Submit to God. Resist the devil and he will flee from you.

Humble yourselves in the sight of the Lord, and He will lift you up.

JAMES 4:7, 10

Walk worthy of the calling with which you were called, with all lowliness and gentleness.

EPHESIANS 4:1

Let the word of Christ dwell in you richly in all wisdom, teaching and admonishing one another in psalms and hymns and spiritual songs, singing with grace in your hearts to the Lord.

COLOSSIANS 3:16

Then he said to them, "Go your way, eat the fat, drink the sweet, and send portions to those for whom nothing is prepared; for this day is holy to our LORD. Do not sorrow, for the joy of the LORD is your strength."

NEHEMIAH 8:10

Those who sow in tears
Shall reap in joy.
He who continually goes forth weeping,
Bearing seed for sowing,
Shall doubtless come again with rejoicing,
Bringing his sheaves with him.

PSALM 126:5–6

Restore to me the joy of Your salvation,
And uphold me by Your generous Spirit.

Then I will teach transgressors Your ways,
And sinners shall be converted to You.

PSALM 51:12–13

This is the day the LORD has made;
We will rejoice and be glad in it.

PSALM 118:24

His lord said to him, "Well done, good and faithful
servant; you were faithful over a few things, I will
make you ruler over many things. Enter into the joy
of your lord."

MATTHEW 25:21

These things I have spoken to you, that My joy may
remain in you, and that your joy may be full. This is
My commandment, that you love one another as I
have loved you.

JOHN 15:11–12

You became followers of us and of the Lord, having
received the word in much affliction, with joy of the
Holy Spirit.

1 THESSALONIANS 1:6

My lips shall greatly rejoice when I sing to You, and
my soul, which You have redeemed.

PSALM 71:23

GOD REJOICES WITH
WOMEN WHEN
THEY . . .

You call me Teacher and Lord, and you say well, for so
I am. If I then, your Lord and Teacher, have washed
your feet, you also ought to wash one another's feet.
For I have given you an example, that you should do
as I have done to you. Most assuredly, I say to you, a
servant is not greater than his master; nor is he who is
sent greater than he who sent him. If you know these
things, blessed are you if you do them.

JOHN 13:13–17

God is faithful, by whom you were called into the fellowship of His Son, Jesus Christ our Lord.

Now I plead with you, brethren, by the name of
our Lord Jesus Christ, that you all speak the same
thing, and that there be no divisions among you, but
that you be perfectly joined together in the same mind
and in the same judgment.

1 CORINTHIANS 1:9–10

*God's Promises*

God, who is rich in mercy, because of His great love with which He loved us, even when we were dead in trespasses, made us alive together with Christ (by grace you have been saved), and raised us up together, and made us sit together in the heavenly places in Christ Jesus.

EPHESIANS 2:4–6

Now John answered Him, saying, "Teacher, we saw someone who does not follow us casting out demons in Your name, and we forbade him because he does not follow us."

But Jesus said, "Do not forbid him, for no one who works a miracle in My name can soon afterward speak evil of Me. For he who is not against us is on our side. For whoever gives you a cup of water to drink in My name, because you belong to Christ, assuredly, I say to you, he will by no means lose his reward.

But whoever causes one of these little ones who believe in Me to stumble, it would be better for him if a millstone were hung around his neck, and he were thrown into the sea."

MARK 9:38–42

He who says he is in the light, and hates his brother, is in darkness until now. He who loves his brother abides in the light, and there is no cause for stumbling in him. But he who hates his brother is in darkness and walks in darkness, and does not know where he is going, because the darkness has blinded his eyes.

1 JOHN 2:9–11

You are a chosen generation, a royal priesthood, a holy nation, His own special people, that you may proclaim the praises of Him who called you out of darkness into His marvelous light.

1 PETER 2:9

If we say that we have fellowship with Him, and walk in darkness, we lie and do not practice the truth. But if we walk in the light as He is in the light, we have fellowship with one another, and the blood of Jesus Christ His Son cleanses us from all sin.

1 JOHN 1:6–7

Now indeed there are many members, yet one body. And the eye cannot say to the hand, "I have no need of you"; nor again the head to the feet, "I have no need of you." No, much rather, those members of the body which seem to be weaker are necessary. And those members of the body which we think to be less honorable, on these we bestow greater honor; and our unpresentable parts have greater modesty, but our presentable parts have no need. But God composed the body, having given greater honor to that part which lacks it, that there should be no schism in the body, but that the members should have the same care for one another. And if one member suffers, all the members suffer with it; or if one member is honored, all the members rejoice with it.

Now you are the body of Christ, and members individually.

1 CORINTHIANS 12:20–27

Forsake foolishness and live,
And go in the way of understanding.
The fear of the LORD is the beginning of
wisdom,
And the knowledge of the Holy One
is understanding.

PROVERBS 9:6, 10

How much better to get wisdom than gold!
And to get understanding is to be
chosen rather than silver.
The highway of the upright is to depart
from evil;
He who keeps his way preserves his soul.

PROVERBS 16:16–17

Seek the LORD while He may be found,
Call upon Him while He is near.
"For My thoughts are not your thoughts,
Nor are your ways My ways," says the LORD.
For as the heavens are higher than the earth,
So are My ways higher than your ways,
And My thoughts than your thoughts.

ISAIAH 55:6, 8–9

If any of you lacks wisdom, let him ask of God, who gives to all liberally and without reproach, and it will be given to him.

JAMES 1:5

> Make me understand the way of Your
>      precepts;
> So shall I meditate on Your wonderful works.
> Give me understanding, and I shall
>      keep Your law;
> Indeed, I shall observe it with my
>      whole heart.
> Your hands have made me and fashioned me;
> Give me understanding, that I may
>      learn Your commandments.
> You, through Your commandments,
>      make me wiser than my enemies;
> For they are ever with me.
> Through Your precepts I get understanding;
> Therefore I hate every false way.
> Your word is a lamp to my feet
> And a light to my path.
> I am Your servant;
> Give me understanding,
> That I may know Your testimonies.
>      PSALM 119:27, 34, 73, 98, 104–105, 125

*God's Promises*

But there is a spirit in man,
And the breath of the Almighty gives him
understanding.

JOB 32:8


Great is our Lord, and mighty in power;
His understanding is infinite.

PSALM 147:5


For the LORD gives wisdom;
From His mouth come knowledge
and understanding;
He stores up sound wisdom for the upright;
He is a shield to those who walk uprightly.

PROVERBS 2:6–7


Lead me in Your truth and teach me, for You are the
God of my salvation.

PSALM 25:5


I applied my heart to know, to search and seek out
wisdom and the reason for things.

ECCLESIASTES 7:25

If you seek her as silver,
And search for her as for hidden treasures;
Then you will understand the fear of
     the LORD,
And find the knowledge of God.

PROVERBS 2:4–5

He does not delight in the strength of
     the horse;
He takes no pleasure in the legs of a man.
The LORD takes pleasure in those who fear Him,
In those who hope in His mercy.

PSALM 147:10–11

The fear of the LORD is the beginning
     of knowledge,
But fools despise wisdom and instruction.

PROVERBS 1:7

The fear of the LORD leads to life,
And he who has it will abide in satisfaction;
He will not be visited with evil.

PROVERBS 19:23

In the fear of the LORD there is strong
     confidence,
And His children will have a place of refuge.
The fear of the LORD is a fountain of life,
To turn one away from the snares of death.

PROVERBS 14:26–27

Then those who feared the LORD spoke
     to one another,
And the LORD listened and heard them;
So a book of remembrance was
     written before Him
For those who fear the LORD
And who meditate on His name.
"They shall be Mine," says the LORD
     of hosts,
"On the day that I make them My jewels.
And I will spare them
As a man spares his own son who serves him."

MALACHI 3:16–17

In mercy and truth
Atonement is provided for iniquity;
And by the fear of the LORD one
     departs from evil.

PROVERBS 16:6

Let us hear the conclusion of the whole matter:
Fear God and keep His commandments,
For this is man's all.
For God will bring every work into
     judgment,
Including every secret thing,
Whether good or evil.

ECCLESIASTES 12:13–14

Praise the LORD!
Blessed is the man who fears the LORD,
Who delights greatly in His commandments.

PSALM 112:1

Who is the man that fears the LORD?
Him shall He teach in the way He chooses.
He himself shall dwell in prosperity,
And his descendants shall inherit the earth.
The secret of the LORD is with those who
     fear Him,
And He will show them His covenant.

PSALM 25:12–14

Behold, the fear of the Lord, that is wisdom,
And to depart from evil is understanding.

JOB 28:28

For the LORD is our Judge,
The LORD is our Lawgiver,
The LORD is our King;
He will save us.

ISAIAH 33:22

Then Moses said to God, "Indeed, when I come to the children of Israel and say to them, 'The God of your fathers has sent me to you,' and they say to me, 'What is His name?' what shall I say to them?"

And God said to Moses, "I AM WHO I AM." And He said, "Thus you shall say to the children of Israel, 'I AM has sent me to you.'"

EXODUS 3:13–14

For with God nothing will be impossible.

LUKE 1:37

The heavens declare the glory of God;
And the firmament shows His handiwork.

PSALM 19:1

Behold, I am the LORD, the God of all flesh. Is there anything too hard for Me?

JEREMIAH 32:27


Great is the LORD, and greatly to be praised;
And His greatness is unsearchable.
One generation shall praise Your works
to another,
And shall declare Your mighty acts.
Your kingdom is an everlasting kingdom,
And Your dominion endures throughout
all generations.

PSALM 145:3–4, 13


Whom have I in heaven but You?
And there is none upon earth that I
desire besides You.

PSALM 73:25


For thus says the High and Lofty One
Who inhabits eternity, whose name is Holy:
"I dwell in the high and holy place,
With him who has a contrite and
humble spirit,
To revive the spirit of the humble,
And to revive the heart of the contrite ones."

ISAIAH 57:15

In the beginning God created the heavens and the earth. The earth was without form, and void; and darkness was on the face of the deep. And the Spirit of God was hovering over the face of the waters. Then God said, "Let there be light"; and there was light.

GENESIS 1:1–3

> "Am I a God near at hand," says the LORD,
> "And not a God afar off?
>   Can anyone hide himself in secret places,
>   So I shall not see him?" says the LORD;
> "Do I not fill heaven and earth?" says
>       the LORD.

JEREMIAH 23:23–24

For of Him and through Him and to Him are all things, to whom be glory forever.

ROMANS 11:36

For your light has come!
And the glory of the LORD is risen upon you.
For behold, the darkness shall cover
    the earth,
And deep darkness the people;
But the LORD will arise over you,
And His glory will be seen upon you.

ISAIAH 60:1–2

All the ends of the world
Shall remember and turn to the LORD,
And all the families of the nations
Shall worship before You.
For the kingdom is the LORD's,
And He rules over the nations.

PSALM 22:27–28

For the earth will be filled
With the knowledge of the glory of the LORD,
As the waters cover the sea.

HABAKKUK 2:14

This gospel of the kingdom will be preached in all the world as a witness to all the nations, and then the end will come.

MATTHEW 24:14

> The voice of one crying in the wilderness:
> "Prepare the way of the LORD;
> Make straight in the desert
> A highway for our God.
> Every valley shall be exalted
> And every mountain and hill brought low;
> The crooked places shall be made straight
> And the rough places smooth;
> The glory of the LORD shall be revealed,
> And all flesh shall see it together;
> For the mouth of the LORD has spoken."

ISAIAH 40:3–5

I will seek what was lost and bring back what was driven away, bind up the broken and strengthen what was sick; but I will destroy the fat and the strong, and feed them in judgment.

EZEKIEL 34:16

## God's Promises

The LORD has made bare His holy arm
In the eyes of all the nations;
And all the ends of the earth shall see
The salvation of our God.
So shall He sprinkle many nations.
Kings shall shut their mouths at Him;
For what had not been told them they
       shall see,
And what they had not heard they shall
       consider.

ISAIAH 52:10, 15


Indeed the LORD has proclaimed
To the end of the world:
"Say to the daughter of Zion,
'Surely your salvation is coming;
Behold, His reward is with Him,
And His work before Him.'"
And they shall call them The Holy People,
The Redeemed of the LORD;
And you shall be called Sought Out,
A City Not Forsaken.

ISAIAH 62:11–12

I will show wonders in the heavens and in
    the earth:
Blood and fire and pillars of smoke.
The sun shall be turned into darkness,
And the moon into blood,
Before the coming of the great and awesome
    day of the LORD.
And it shall come to pass
That whoever calls on the name of the LORD
Shall be saved.
For in Mount Zion and in Jerusalem
    there shall be deliverance,
As the LORD has said,
Among the remnant whom the LORD calls.

JOEL 2:30–32

Heaven and earth will pass away, but My words will by no means pass away.

MATTHEW 24:35

The Spirit expressly says that in latter times some will depart from the faith, giving heed to deceiving spirits and doctrines of demons, speaking lies in hypocrisy, having their own conscience seared with a hot iron, forbidding to marry, and commanding to abstain from foods which God created to be received with thanksgiving by those who believe and know the truth.

1 TIMOTHY 4:1–3

Know this, that in the last days perilous times will come: For men will be lovers of themselves, lovers of money, boasters, proud, blasphemers, disobedient to parents, unthankful, unholy, unloving, unforgiving, slanderers, without self-control, brutal, despisers of good, traitors, headstrong, haughty, lovers of pleasure rather than lovers of God, having a form of godliness but denying its power. And from such people turn away!

2 TIMOTHY 3:1–5

For since the beginning of the world
Men have not heard nor perceived by the ear,
Nor has the eye seen any God besides You,
Who acts for the one who waits for Him.

ISAIAH 64:4

Jesus answered and said to them: "Take heed that no one deceives you. For many will come in My name, saying, 'I am the Christ,' and will deceive many. And you will hear of wars and rumors of wars. See that you are not troubled; for all these things must come to pass, but the end is not yet. For nation will rise against nation, and kingdom against kingdom. And there will be famines, pestilences, and earthquakes in various places.

All these are the beginning of sorrows. Then they will deliver you up to tribulation and kill you, and you will be hated by all nations for My name's sake. And then many will be offended, will betray one another, and will hate one another. Then many false prophets will rise up and deceive many. And because lawlessness will abound, the love of many will grow cold. But he who endures to the end shall be saved. And this gospel of the kingdom will be preached in all the world as a witness to all the nations, and then the end will come."

MATTHEW 24:4–14

For the wages of sin is death, but the gift of God is
eternal life in Christ Jesus our Lord.

ROMANS 6:23

> And it shall come to pass in the last days,
>     says God,
> That I will pour out of My Spirit on all flesh;
> Your sons and your daughters shall prophesy,
> Your young men shall see visions,
> Your old men shall dream dreams.
> And on My menservants and on My
>     maidservants
> I will pour out My Spirit in those days;
> And they shall prophesy.
> I will show wonders in heaven above
> And signs in the earth beneath:
> Blood and fire and vapor of smoke.
> The sun shall be turned into darkness,
> And the moon into blood,
> Before the coming of the great and
>     awesome day of the LORD.
> And it shall come to pass
> That whoever calls on the name of the LORD
> Shall be saved.

Acts 2:17–21

Then two men will be in the field: one will be taken and the other left.

Watch therefore, for you do not know what hour your Lord is coming.

Therefore you also be ready, for the Son of Man is coming at an hour you do not expect.

MATTHEW 24:40, 42, 44

Behold, I tell you a mystery: We shall not all sleep, but we shall all be changed—in a moment, in the twinkling of an eye, at the last trumpet. For the trumpet will sound, and the dead will be raised incorruptible, and we shall be changed. For this corruptible must put on incorruption, and this mortal must put on immortality. So when this corruptible has put on incorruption, and this mortal has put on immortality, then shall be brought to pass the saying that is written: Death is swallowed up in victory.

O Death, where is your sting?

O Hades, where is your victory?

The sting of death is sin, and the strength of sin is the law. But thanks be to God, who gives us the victory through our Lord Jesus Christ.

1 CORINTHIANS 15:51–57

There are also celestial bodies and terrestrial bodies; but the glory of the celestial is one, and the glory of the terrestrial is another.

So also is the resurrection of the dead. The body is sown in corruption, it is raised in incorruption. It is sown in dishonor, it is raised in glory. It is sown in weakness, it is raised in power. It is sown a natural body, it is raised a spiritual body. There is a natural body, and there is a spiritual body.

1 CORINTHIANS 15:40, 42–44

Beloved, now we are children of God; and it has not yet been revealed what we shall be, but we know that when He is revealed, we shall be like Him, for we shall see Him as He is. And everyone who has this hope in Him purifies himself, just as He is pure.

1 JOHN 3:2–3

I do not want you to be ignorant, brethren, concerning those who have fallen asleep, lest you sorrow as others who have no hope. For if we believe that Jesus died and rose again, even so God will bring with Him those who sleep in Jesus.

For this we say to you by the word of the Lord, that we who are alive and remain until the coming of the Lord will by no means precede those who are asleep. For the Lord Himself will descend from heaven with a shout, with the voice of an archangel, and with the trumpet of God. And the dead in Christ will rise first. Then we who are alive and remain shall be caught up together with them in the clouds to meet the Lord in the air. And thus we shall always be with the Lord. Therefore comfort one another with these words.

1 THESSALONIANS 4:13–18

# DYNAMIC WOMEN OF FAITH . . .

Now in the sixth month the angel Gabriel was sent by God to a city of Galilee named Nazareth, to a virgin betrothed to a man whose name was Joseph, of the house of David. The virgin's name was Mary. And having come in, the angel said to her, "Rejoice, highly favored one, the Lord is with you; blessed are you among women!"

But when she saw him, she was troubled at his saying, and considered what manner of greeting this was. Then the angel said to her, "Do not be afraid, Mary, for you have found favor with God. And behold, you will conceive in your womb and bring forth a Son, and shall call His name JESUS."

LUKE 1:26–31

Now there stood by the cross of Jesus His mother, and His mother's sister, Mary the wife of Clopas, and Mary Magdalene. When Jesus therefore saw His mother, and the disciple whom He loved standing by, He said to His mother, "Woman, behold your son!" Then He said to the disciple, "Behold your mother!" And from that hour that disciple took her to his own home.

JOHN 19:25–27

And Mary said:
"My soul magnifies the Lord,
And my spirit has rejoiced in God my Savior.
For He has regarded the lowly state of
     His maidservant;
For behold, henceforth all generations
     will call me blessed.
For He who is mighty has done great
     things for me,
And holy is His name.
And His mercy is on those who fear Him
From generation to generation.
He has shown strength with His arm;
He has scattered the proud in the
     imagination of their hearts.
He has put down the mighty from
     their thrones,
And exalted the lowly.
He has filled the hungry with good things,
And the rich He has sent away empty."

LUKE 1:46–53

There was in the days of Herod, the king of Judea, a
certain priest named Zacharias, of the division of
Abijah. His wife was of the daughters of Aaron, and
her name was Elizabeth. And they were both righteous
before God, walking in all the commandments and
ordinances of the Lord blameless. But they had no
child, because Elizabeth was barren, and they were
both well advanced in years.

LUKE 1:5–7

The angel said to him, "Do not be afraid, Zacharias,
for your prayer is heard; and your wife Elizabeth will
bear you a son, and you shall call his name John."

LUKE 1:13

Now indeed, Elizabeth your relative has also conceived a son in her old age; and this is now the sixth
month for her who was called barren. For with God
nothing will be impossible.

LUKE 1:36–37

You, child, will be called the prophet of
    the Highest;
For you will go before the face of the Lord
    to prepare His ways,
To give knowledge of salvation to His people
By the remission of their sins.

LUKE 1:76–77

It happened, when Elizabeth heard the greeting of Mary, that the babe leaped in her womb; and Elizabeth was filled with the Holy Spirit. Then she spoke out with a loud voice and said, "Blessed are you among women, and blessed is the fruit of your womb! But why is this granted to me, that the mother of my Lord should come to me? For indeed, as soon as the voice of your greeting sounded in my ears, the babe leaped in my womb for joy. Blessed is she who believed, for there will be a fulfillment of those things which were told her from the Lord."

LUKE 1:41–45

# Dynamic Women of Faith . . . Sarah—
## Wife of Abraham

Then God said to Abraham, "As for Sarai your wife, you shall not call her name Sarai, but Sarah shall be her name. And I will bless her and also give you a son by her; then I will bless her, and she shall be a mother of nations; kings of peoples shall be from her."

GENESIS 17:15–16

Then God said: "No, Sarah your wife shall bear you a son, and you shall call his name Isaac; I will establish My covenant with him for an everlasting covenant, and with his descendants after him."

GENESIS 17:19

The LORD visited Sarah as He had said, and the LORD did for Sarah as He had spoken. For Sarah conceived and bore Abraham a son in his old age, at the set time of which God had spoken to him. And Abraham called the name of his son who was born to him—whom Sarah bore to him—Isaac.

GENESIS 21:1–3

God said to Abraham, "Do not let it be displeasing in your sight because of the lad or because of your bond-woman. Whatever Sarah has said to you, listen to her voice; for in Isaac your seed shall be called."

GENESIS 21:12

By faith Sarah herself also received strength to conceive seed, and she bore a child when she was was past the age, because she judged Him faithful who had promised.

HEBREWS 11:11

She was in bitterness of soul, and prayed to the LORD and wept in anguish. Then she made a vow and said, "O LORD of hosts, if You will indeed look on the affliction of Your maidservant and remember me, and not forget Your maidservant, but will give Your maidservant a male child, then I will give him to the LORD all the days of his life, and no razor shall come upon his head."

1 SAMUEL 1:10–11

It came to pass in the process of time that Hannah conceived and bore a son, and called his name Samuel, saying, "Because I have asked for him from the LORD."

1 SAMUEL 1:20

The LORD has granted me my petition which I asked of Him. Therefore I also have lent him to the LORD; as long as he lives he shall be lent to the LORD. So they worshiped the LORD there.

1 SAMUEL 1:27–28

The LORD visited Hannah, so that she conceived and bore three sons and two daughters. Meanwhile the child Samuel grew before the LORD.

1 SAMUEL 2:21

Boaz answered and said to her, "It has been fully reported to me, all that you have done for your mother-in-law since the death of your husband, and how you have left your father and your mother and the land of your birth, and have come to a people whom you did not know before. The LORD repay your work, and a full reward be given you by the LORD God of Israel, under whose wings you have come for refuge."

Then she said, "Let me find favor in your sight, my lord; for you have comforted me, and have spoken kindly to your maidservant, though I am not like one of your maidservants."

RUTH 2:11–13

Blessed are you of the LORD, my daughter! For you have shown more kindness at the end than at the beginning, in that you did not go after young men, whether poor or rich. And now, my daughter, do not fear. I will do for you all that you request, for all the people of my town know that you are a virtuous woman.

RUTH 3:10–11

So Boaz took Ruth and she became his wife; and when he went in to her, the LORD gave her conception, and she bore a son.

RUTH 4:13

The neighbor women gave him a name, saying, "There is a son born to Naomi." And they called his name Obed. He is the father of Jesse, the father of David.

RUTH 4:17

# Dynamic Women of Faith . . . Lydia—Seller of Purple (Merchant)

On the Sabbath day we went out of the city to the riverside, where prayer was customarily made; and we sat down and spoke to the women who met there. Now a certain woman named Lydia heard us. She was a seller of purple from the city of Thyatira, who worshiped God. The Lord opened her heart to heed the things spoken by Paul. And when she and her household were baptized, she begged us, saying, "If you have judged me to be faithful to the Lord, come to my house and stay." So she persuaded us.

ACTS 16:13–15

When it was day, the magistrates sent the officers, saying, "Let those men go."

So they went out of the prison and entered the house of Lydia; and when they had seen the brethren, they encouraged them and departed.

ACTS 16:35, 40

# GOD'S ANSWERS
# FOR WOMEN

# Beginning in Christ

If you confess with your mouth the Lord Jesus and believe in your heart that God has raised Him from the dead, you will be saved.

For with the heart one believes unto righteousness, and with the mouth confession is made unto salvation.

For the Scripture says, "Whoever believes on Him will not be put to shame."

ROMANS 10:9–11

Most assuredly, I say to you, he who hears My word and believes in Him who sent Me has everlasting life, and shall not come into judgment, but has passed from death into life.

JOHN 5:24

You are all sons of God through faith in Christ Jesus.

For as many of you as were baptized into Christ have put on Christ.

There is neither Jew nor Greek, there is neither slave nor free, there is neither male nor female; for you are all one in Christ Jesus.

GALATIANS 3:26–28

If anyone is in Christ, he is a new creation; old things have passed away; behold, all things have become new.

2 CORINTHIANS 5:17

Whoever confesses Me before men, him I will also confess before My Father who is in heaven.

And he who does not take his cross and follow after Me is not worthy of Me.

He who finds his life will lose it, and he who loses his life for My sake will find it.

MATTHEW 10:32, 38–39

I have been crucified with Christ; it is no longer I who live, but Christ lives in me; and the life which I now live in the flesh I live by faith in the Son of God, who loved me and gave Himself for me.

GALATIANS 2:20

Having been born again, not of corruptible seed but incorruptible, through the word of God which lives and abides forever.

1 PETER 1:23

We know that we have passed from death to life, because we love the brethren. He who does not love his brother abides in death.

1 JOHN 3:14

Those who are Christ's have crucified the flesh with its passions and desires.

If we live in the Spirit, let us also walk in the Spirit.

GALATIANS 5:24–25

I will give you a new heart and put a new spirit within you; I will take the heart of stone out of your flesh and give you a heart of flesh.

I will put My Spirit within you and cause you to walk in My statutes, and you will keep My judgments and do them.

EZEKIEL 36:26–27

He who received seed on the good ground is he who hears the word and understands it, who indeed bears fruit and produces: some a hundredfold, some sixty, some thirty.

MATTHEW 13:23

Knowing this, that our old man was crucified with Him, that the body of sin might be done away with, that we should no longer be slaves of sin.

For he who has died has been freed from sin.

Now if we died with Christ, we believe that we shall also live with Him.

ROMANS 6:6–8

Looking unto Jesus, the author and finisher of our faith, who for the joy that was set before Him endured the cross, despising the shame, and has sat down at the right hand of the throne of God.

HEBREWS 12:2

Jesus said to them, "I am the bread of life. He who comes to Me shall never hunger, and he who believes in Me shall never thirst."

JOHN 6:35

Let your conduct be without covetousness; be content with such things as you have. For He Himself has said, "I will never leave you nor forsake you."

So we may boldly say: "The LORD is my helper; I will not fear. What can man do to me?"

Jesus Christ is the same yesterday, today, and forever.

HEBREWS 13:5–6, 8

If the Son makes you free, you shall be free indeed.

JOHN 8:36

213

*God's Answers*

I can do all things through Christ who strengthens me.

PHILIPPIANS 4:13

For in Him dwells all the fullness of the Godhead bodily; and you are complete in Him, who is the head of all principality and power.

COLOSSIANS 2:9–10

I am the good shepherd. The good shepherd gives His life for the sheep.

JOHN 10:11

> The LORD is my shepherd;
> I shall not want.
> He makes me to lie down in green pastures;
> He leads me beside the still waters.
> He restores my soul;
> He leads me in the paths of righteousness
> For His name's sake.
> Yea, though I walk through the valley of the
>       shadow of death,
> I will fear no evil;
> For You are with me;
> Your rod and Your staff, they comfort me.

PSALM 23:1–4

We have such trust through Christ toward God.

Not that we are sufficient of ourselves to think of anything as being from ourselves, but our sufficiency is from God.

2 CORINTHIANS 3:4–5

The Lord stood with me and strengthened me, so that the message might be preached fully through me, and that all the Gentiles might hear. And I was delivered out of the mouth of the lion.

And the Lord will deliver me from every evil work and preserve me for His heavenly kingdom. To Him be glory forever and ever. Amen!

2 TIMOTHY 4:17–18

My help comes from the LORD,
Who made heaven and earth.
He will not allow your foot to be moved;
He who keeps you will not slumber.

PSALM 121:2–3

Jesus said to him, "I am the way, the truth, and the life. No one comes to the Father except through Me."

JOHN 14:6

This is My blood of the new covenant, which is shed for many for the remission of sins.

MATTHEW 26:28

Being justified freely by His grace through the redemption that is in Christ Jesus, whom God set forth as a propitiation by His blood, through faith, to demonstrate His righteousness, because in His forbearance God had passed over the sins that were previously committed, to demonstrate at the present time His righteousness, that He might be just and the justifier of the one who has faith in Jesus.

ROMANS 3:24–26

For the life of the flesh is in the blood, and I have given it to you upon the altar to make atonement for your souls; for it is the blood that makes atonement for the soul.

LEVITICUS 17:11

How much more shall the blood of Christ, who through the eternal Spirit offered Himself without spot to God, cleanse your conscience from dead works to serve the living God?

HEBREWS 9:14

God demonstrates His own love toward us, in that while we were still sinners, Christ died for us.

Much more then, having now been justified by His blood, we shall be saved from wrath through Him.

For if when we were enemies we were reconciled to God through the death of His Son, much more, having been reconciled, we shall be saved by His life.

ROMANS 5:8–10

If we walk in the light as He is in the light, we have fellowship with one another, and the blood of Jesus Christ His Son cleanses us from all sin.

1 JOHN 1:7

Then Jesus said to them, "Most assuredly, I say to you, unless you eat the flesh of the Son of Man and drink His blood, you have no life in you.

"Whoever eats My flesh and drinks My blood has eternal life, and I will raise him up at the last day.

"He who eats My flesh and drinks My blood abides in Me, and I in him."

JOHN 6:53, 54, 56

In Him we have redemption through His blood, the forgiveness of sins, according to the riches of His grace.

EPHESIANS 1:7

Then likewise he sprinkled with blood both the tabernacle and all the vessels of the ministry.

And according to the law almost all things are purified with blood, and without shedding of blood there is no remission.

HEBREWS 9:21–22

Knowing that you were not redeemed with corruptible things, like silver or gold, from your aimless conduct received by tradition from your fathers, but with the precious blood of Christ, as of a lamb without blemish and without spot.

He indeed was foreordained before the foundation of the world, but was manifest in these last times for you who through Him believe in God, who raised Him from the dead and gave Him glory, so that your faith and hope are in God.

1 PETER 1:18–21

The word of God is living and powerful, and sharper than any two-edged sword, piercing even to the division of soul and spirit, and of joints and marrow, and is a discerner of the thoughts and intents of the heart.

HEBREWS 4:12

By the word of the LORD the heavens were made, and all the host of them by the breath of His mouth.

PSALM 33:6

Your word I have hidden in my heart, that I might not sin against You!

I will delight myself in Your statutes; I will not forget Your word.

PSALM 119:11, 16

How sweet are Your words to my taste,
Sweeter than honey to my mouth!
Through Your precepts I get understanding;
Therefore I hate every false way.
Your word is a lamp to my feet
And a light to my path.

PSALM 119:103–105

219

Forever, O Lᴏʀᴅ,
Your word is settled in heaven.
Your faithfulness endures to all generations;
You established the earth, and it abides.

PSALM 119:89–90


Your testimonies are wonderful;
Therefore my soul keeps them.
The entrance of Your words gives light;
It gives understanding to the simple.

PSALM 119:29–30


As newborn babes, desire the pure milk of the word,
that you may grow thereby, if indeed you have tasted
that the Lord is gracious.

1 PETER 2:2–3


You are already clean because of the word which I
have spoken to you.

JOHN 15:3


The grass withers, the flower fades, but the word of
our God stands forever.

ISAIAH 40:8


Heaven and earth will pass away, but My words will
by no means pass away.

LUKE 21:33

He answered and said, "It is written, 'Man shall not live by bread alone, but by every word that proceeds from the mouth of God.'"

MATTHEW 4:4

Having been born again, not of corruptible seed but incorruptible, through the word of God which lives and abides forever, because "All flesh is as grass, and all the glory of man as the flower of the grass. The grass withers, and its flower falls away, but the word of the LORD endures forever."

Now this is the word which by the gospel was preached to you.

1 PETER 1:23–25

It is the Spirit who gives life; the flesh profits nothing. The words that I speak to you are spirit, and they are life.

JOHN 6:63

Then Jesus said to those Jews who believed Him, "If you abide in My word, you are My disciples indeed.

"And you shall know the truth, and the truth shall make you free."

JOHN 8:31–32

And being assembled together with them, He commanded them not to depart from Jerusalem, but to wait for the Promise of the Father, "which," He said, "you have heard from Me; "for John truly baptized with water, but you shall be baptized with the Holy Spirit not many days from now."

Therefore, when they had come together, they asked Him, saying, "Lord, will You at this time restore the kingdom to Israel?"

And He said to them, "It is not for you to know times or seasons which the Father has put in His own authority.

"But you shall receive power when the Holy Spirit has come upon you; and you shall be witnesses to Me in Jerusalem, and in all Judea and Samaria, and to the end of the earth."

ACTS 1:4–8

See that you do not refuse Him who speaks. For if they did not escape who refused Him who spoke on earth, much more shall we not escape if we turn away from Him who speaks from heaven.

HEBREWS 12:25

But the fruit of the Spirit is love, joy, peace, longsuf-fering, kindness, goodness, faithfulness, gentleness, self-control. Against such there is no law.

And those who are Christ's have crucified the flesh with its passions and desires.

If we live in the Spirit, let us also walk in the Spirit.

GALATIANS 5:22–25

It is not you who speak, but the Spirit of your Father who speaks in you.

MATTHEW 10:20

So shall they fear
The name of the LORD from the west,
And His glory from the rising of the sun;
When the enemy comes in like a flood,
The Spirit of the LORD will lift up a standard
against him.

ISAIAH 59:19

The Holy Spirit will teach you in that very hour what you ought to say.

LUKE 12:12

Do not grieve the Holy Spirit of God, by whom you were sealed for the day of redemption.

EPHESIANS 4:30

Who also made us sufficient as ministers of the new covenant, not of the letter but of the Spirit; for the letter kills, but the Spirit gives life.

Now the Lord is the Spirit; and where the Spirit of the Lord is, there is liberty.

But we all, with unveiled face, beholding as in a mirror the glory of the Lord, are being transformed into the same image from glory to glory, just as by the Spirit of the Lord.

2 CORINTHIANS 3:6, 17–18

Knowing this first, that no prophecy of Scripture is of any private interpretation, for prophecy never came by the will of man, but holy men of God spoke as they were moved by the Holy Spirit.

2 PETER 1:20–21

But you, beloved, building yourselves up on your most holy faith, praying in the Holy Spirit, keep yourselves in the love of God, looking for the mercy of our Lord Jesus Christ unto eternal life.

JUDE 20, 21

Behold, I send the Promise of My Father upon you; but tarry in the city of Jerusalem until you are endued with power from on high.

LUKE 24:49

Abide in Me, and I in you. As the branch cannot bear fruit of itself, unless it abides in the vine, neither can you, unless you abide in Me.

I am the vine, you are the branches. He who abides in Me, and I in him, bears much fruit; for without Me you can do nothing.

If anyone does not abide in Me, he is cast out as a branch and is withered; and they gather them and throw them into the fire, and they are burned.

If you abide in Me, and My words abide in you, you will ask what you desire, and it shall be done for you.

JOHN 15:4–7

And now, little children, abide in Him, that when He appears, we may have confidence and not be ashamed before Him at His coming.

1 JOHN 2:28

I love those who love me, and those who seek me diligently will find me.

PROVERBS 8:17

I will meditate on Your precepts,
And contemplate Your ways.
I will delight myself in Your statutes;
I will not forget Your word.

PSALM 119:15–16


Let the word of Christ dwell in you richly in all wisdom, teaching and admonishing one another in psalms and hymns and spiritual songs, singing with grace in your hearts to the Lord.

COLOSSIANS 3:16


Those who wait on the LORD
Shall renew their strength;
They shall mount up with wings like eagles,
They shall run and not be weary,
They shall walk and not faint.

ISAIAH 40:31


Draw near to God and He will draw near to you. Cleanse your hands, you sinners; and purify your hearts, you double-minded.

JAMES 4:8


But put on the Lord Jesus Christ, and make no provision for the flesh, to fulfill its lusts.

ROMANS 13:14

Now by this we know that we know Him, if we keep His commandments.

He who says, "I know Him," and does not keep His commandments, is a liar, and the truth is not in him.

But whoever keeps His word, truly the love of God is perfected in him. By this we know that we are in Him.

He who says he abides in Him ought himself also to walk just as He walked.

1 JOHN 2:3–6

In Him we live and move and have our being, as also some of your own poets have said, "For we are also His offspring."

ACTS 17:28

Blessed is the man who listens to me,
Watching daily at my gates,
Waiting at the posts of my doors.

PROVERBS 8:34

As newborn babes, desire the pure milk of the word, that you may grow thereby.

1 PETER 2:2

But be doers of the word, and not hearers only, deceiving yourselves.

JAMES 1:22

Now faith is the substance of things hoped for, the evidence of things not seen.

By faith we understand that the worlds were framed by the word of God, so that the things which are seen were not made of things which are visible.

But without faith it is impossible to please Him, for he who comes to God must believe that He is, and that He is a rewarder of those who diligently seek Him.

By faith he forsook Egypt, not fearing the wrath of the king; for he endured as seeing Him who is invisible.

HEBREWS 11:1, 3, 6, 27

That the genuineness of your faith, being much more precious than gold that perishes, though it is tested by fire, may be found to praise, honor, and glory at the revelation of Jesus Christ, whom having not seen you love. Though now you do not see Him, yet believing, you rejoice with joy inexpressible and full of glory, receiving the end of your faith—the salvation of your souls.

1 PETER 1:7–9

For with God nothing will be impossible.

LUKE 1:37

For in it the righteousness of God is revealed from faith to faith; as it is written, "The just shall live by faith."

ROMANS 1:17

So then faith comes by hearing, and hearing by the word of God.

ROMANS 10:17

Have I not commanded you? Be strong and of good courage; do not be afraid, nor be dismayed, for the LORD your God is with you wherever you go.

JOSHUA 1:9

If any of you lacks wisdom, let him ask of God, who gives to all liberally and without reproach, and it will be given to him.

But let him ask in faith, with no doubting, for he who doubts is like a wave of the sea driven and tossed by the wind.

For let not that man suppose that he will receive anything from the Lord; he is a double-minded man, unstable in all his ways.

JAMES 1:5–8

He did not waver at the promise of God through unbelief, but was strengthened in faith, giving glory to God, and being fully convinced that what He had promised He was also able to perform.

ROMANS 4:20–21

We are hard pressed on every side, yet not crushed; we are perplexed, but not in despair; persecuted, but not forsaken; struck down, but not destroyed—always carrying about in the body the dying of the Lord Jesus, that the life of Jesus also may be manifested in our body.

2 CORINTHIANS 4:8–10

What then shall we say to these things? If God is for us, who can be against us?

ROMANS 8:31

But you, beloved, building yourselves up on your most holy faith, praying in the Holy Spirit, keep yourselves in the love of God, looking for the mercy of our Lord Jesus Christ unto eternal life.

JUDE 20, 21

We walk by faith, not by sight.

2 CORINTHIANS 5:7

GROWING IN CHRIST

For you, brethren, have been called to liberty; only do not use liberty as an opportunity for the flesh, but through love serve one another.

For all the law is fulfilled in one word, even in this: "You shall love your neighbor as yourself."

But if you bite and devour one another, beware lest you be consumed by one another!

I say then: Walk in the Spirit, and you shall not fulfill the lust of the flesh.

For the flesh lusts against the Spirit, and the Spirit against the flesh; and these are contrary to one another, so that you do not do the things that you wish.

GALATIANS 5:13–17

I beseech you therefore, brethren, by the mercies of God, that you present your bodies a living sacrifice, holy, acceptable to God, which is your reasonable service.

And do not be conformed to this world, but be transformed by the renewing of your mind, that you may prove what is that good and acceptable and perfect will of God.

ROMANS 12:1–2

For the law of the Spirit of life in Christ Jesus has made me free from the law of sin and death.

For what the law could not do in that it was weak through the flesh, God did by sending His own Son in the likeness of sinful flesh, on account of sin: He condemned sin in the flesh, that the righteous requirement of the law might be fulfilled in us who do not walk according to the flesh but according to the Spirit.

For those who live according to the flesh set their minds on the things of the flesh, but those who live according to the Spirit, the things of the Spirit.

For to be carnally minded is death, but to be spiritually minded is life and peace.

Because the carnal mind is enmity against God; for it is not subject to the law of God, nor indeed can be.

So then, those who are in the flesh cannot please God.

But you are not in the flesh but in the Spirit, if indeed the Spirit of God dwells in you. Now if anyone does not have the Spirit of Christ, he is not His.

And if Christ is in you, the body is dead because of sin, but the Spirit is life because of righteousness.

But if the Spirit of Him who raised Jesus from the dead dwells in you, He who raised Christ from the dead will also give life to your mortal bodies through His Spirit who dwells in you.

ROMANS 8:2–11

Who has known the mind of the LORD that he may instruct Him? But we have the mind of Christ.

1 CORINTHIANS 2:16

Therefore gird up the loins of your mind, be sober, and rest your hope fully upon the grace that is to be brought to you at the revelation of Jesus Christ; as obedient children, not conforming yourselves to the former lusts, as in your ignorance; but as He who called you is holy, you also be holy in all your conduct.

1 PETER 1:13–15

I have been crucified with Christ; it is no longer I who live, but Christ lives in me; and the life which I now live in the flesh I live by faith in the Son of God, who loved me and gave Himself for me.

GALATIANS 2:20

Beware lest anyone cheat you through philosophy and empty deceit, according to the tradition of men, according to the basic principles of the world, and not according to Christ.

COLOSSIANS 2:8

Therefore we do not lose heart. Even though our outward man is perishing, yet the inward man is being renewed day by day.

2 CORINTHIANS 4:16

Finally, my brethren, be strong in the Lord and in the power of His might.

Put on the whole armor of God, that you may be able to stand against the wiles of the devil.

For we do not wrestle against flesh and blood, but against principalities, against powers, against the rulers of the darkness of this age, against spiritual hosts of wickedness in the heavenly places.

Therefore take up the whole armor of God, that you may be able to withstand in the evil day, and having done all, to stand.

Stand therefore, having girded your waist with truth, having put on the breastplate of righteousness, and having shod your feet with the preparation of the gospel of peace; above all, taking the shield of faith with which you will be able to quench all the fiery darts of the wicked one.

And take the helmet of salvation, and the sword of the Spirit, which is the word of God.

EPHESIANS 6:10–17

In that He Himself has suffered, being tempted, He is able to aid those who are tempted.

HEBREWS 2:18

Submit to God. Resist the devil and he will flee from you.

Draw near to God and He will draw near to you. Cleanse your hands, you sinners; and purify your hearts, you double-minded.

JAMES 4:7–8

And He said to them, "I saw Satan fall like lightning from heaven. Behold, I give you the authority to trample on serpents and scorpions, and over all the power of the enemy, and nothing shall by any means hurt you."

LUKE 10:18–19

He who sins is of the devil, for the devil has sinned from the beginning. For this purpose the Son of God was manifested, that He might destroy the works of the devil.

1 JOHN 3:8

The LORD shall preserve you from all evil;
He shall preserve your soul.
The LORD shall preserve your going out and
    your coming in
From this time forth, and even forevermore.

PSALM 121:7–8

Be sober, be vigilant; because your adversary the devil walks about like a roaring lion, seeking whom he may devour.

Resist him, steadfast in the faith, knowing that the same sufferings are experienced by your brotherhood in the world.

But may the God of all grace, who called us to His eternal glory by Christ Jesus, after you have suffered a while, perfect, establish, strengthen, and settle you.

1 PETER 5:8–10

Surely He shall deliver you from the snare of
    the fowler
And from the perilous pestilence.
He shall cover you with His feathers,
And under His wings you shall take refuge;
His truth shall be your shield and buckler.
You shall not be afraid of the terror by night,
Nor of the arrow that flies by day,
Nor of the pestilence that walks in darkness,
Nor of the destruction that lays waste at
    noonday.
A thousand may fall at your side,
And ten thousand at your right hand;
But it shall not come near you.

PSALM 91:3–7

# How to Recognize Evil

Beware of false prophets, who come to you in sheep's clothing, but inwardly they are ravenous wolves.

You will know them by their fruits. Do men gather grapes from thornbushes or figs from thistles?

Even so, every good tree bears good fruit, but a bad tree bears bad fruit.

Therefore by their fruits you will know them.

Not everyone who says to Me, "Lord, Lord," shall enter the kingdom of heaven, but he who does the will of My Father in heaven.

Many will say to Me in that day, "Lord, Lord, have we not prophesied in Your name, cast out demons in Your name, and done many wonders in Your name?"

And then I will declare to them, "I never knew you; depart from Me, you who practice lawlessness!"

MATTHEW 7:15–17, 20–23

They profess to know God, but in works they deny Him, being abominable, disobedient, and disqualified for every good work.

TITUS 1:16

Beloved, do not believe every spirit, but test the spirits, whether they are of God; because many false prophets have gone out into the world.

By this you know the Spirit of God: Every spirit that confesses that Jesus Christ has come in the flesh is of God, and every spirit that does not confess that Jesus Christ has come in the flesh is not of God. And this is the spirit of the Antichrist, which you have heard was coming, and is now already in the world.

1 JOHN 4:1–3

And when they say to you, "Seek those who are mediums and wizards, who whisper and mutter," should not a people seek their God? Should they seek the dead on behalf of the living?

To the law and to the testimony! If they do not speak according to this word, it is because there is no light in them.

ISAIAH 8:19–20

Stand fast therefore in the liberty by which Christ has made us free, and do not be entangled again with a yoke of bondage.

GALATIANS 5:1

"Behold, I am against those who prophesy false dreams," says the LORD, "and tell them, and cause My people to err by their lies and by their recklessness. Yet I did not send them or command them; therefore they shall not profit this people at all," says the LORD.

JEREMIAH 23:32

A good tree does not bear bad fruit, nor does a bad tree bear good fruit.

For every tree is known by its own fruit. For men do not gather figs from thorns, nor do they gather grapes from a bramble bush.

LUKE 6:43–44

For God is not the author of confusion but of peace, as in all the churches of the saints.

1 CORINTHIANS 14:33

God has not given us a spirit of fear, but of power and of love and of a sound mind.

2 TIMOTHY 1:7

He who sins is of the devil, for the devil has sinned from the beginning. For this purpose the Son of God was manifested, that He might destroy the works of the devil.

1 JOHN 3:8

No one can serve two masters; for either he will hate the one and love the other, or else he will be loyal to the one and despise the other. You cannot serve God and mammon.

MATTHEW 6:24

Do not love the world or the things in the world. If anyone loves the world, the love of the Father is not in him.

For all that is in the world—the lust of the flesh, the lust of the eyes, and the pride of life—is not of the Father but is of the world.

And the world is passing away, and the lust of it; but he who does the will of God abides forever.

1 JOHN 2:15–17

Do not be conformed to this world, but be transformed by the renewing of your mind, that you may prove what is that good and acceptable and perfect will of God.

ROMANS 12:2

Have no fellowship with the unfruitful works of darkness, but rather expose them.

EPHESIANS 5:11

And do this, knowing the time, that now it is high time to awake out of sleep; for now our salvation is nearer than when we first believed.

The night is far spent, the day is at hand. Therefore let us cast off the works of darkness, and let us put on the armor of light.

Let us walk properly, as in the day, not in revelry and drunkenness, not in lewdness and lust, not in strife and envy.

But put on the Lord Jesus Christ, and make no provision for the flesh, to fulfill its lusts.

ROMANS 13:11–14

The Lord knows how to deliver the godly out of temptations and to reserve the unjust under punishment for the day of judgment.

2 PETER 2:9

Then He said to them all, "If anyone desires to come after Me, let him deny himself, and take up his cross daily, and follow Me.

"For whoever desires to save his life will lose it, but whoever loses his life for My sake will save it.

"For what profit is it to a man if he gains the whole world, and is himself destroyed or lost?"

LUKE 9:23–25

Now therefore, fear the LORD, serve Him in sincerity and in truth, and put away the gods which your fathers served on the other side of the River and in Egypt. Serve the LORD!

JOSHUA 24:14

Choosing rather to suffer affliction with the people of God than to enjoy the passing pleasures of sin, esteeming the reproach of Christ greater riches than the treasures in Egypt; for he looked to the reward.

By faith he forsook Egypt, not fearing the wrath of the king; for he endured as seeing Him who is invisible.

HEBREWS 11:25–27

By which have been given to us exceedingly great and precious promises, that through these you may be partakers of the divine nature, having escaped the corruption that is in the world through lust.

2 PETER 1:4

Take heed to yourselves, lest your hearts be weighed down with carousing, drunkenness, and cares of this life, and that Day come on you unexpectedly.

LUKE 21:34

Do you not know that your bodies are members of Christ? Shall I then take the members of Christ and make them members of a harlot? Certainly not!

Or do you not know that he who is joined to a harlot is one body with her? For "the two," He says, "shall become one flesh."

But he who is joined to the Lord is one spirit with Him.

Flee sexual immorality. Every sin that a man does is outside the body, but he who commits sexual immorality sins against his own body.

Or do you not know that your body is the temple of the Holy Spirit who is in you, whom you have from God, and you are not your own?

For you were bought at a price; therefore glorify God in your body and in your spirit, which are God's.

1 CORINTHIANS 6:15–20

I say then: Walk in the Spirit, and you shall not fulfill the lust of the flesh.

For the flesh lusts against the Spirit, and the Spirit against the flesh; and these are contrary to one another, so that you do not do the things that you wish.

GALATIANS 5:16–17

No temptation has overtaken you except such as is common to man; but God is faithful, who will not allow you to be tempted beyond what you are able, but with the temptation will also make the way of escape, that you may be able to bear it.

1 CORINTHIANS 10:13

Put off, concerning your former conduct, the old man which grows corrupt according to the deceitful lusts, and be renewed in the spirit of your mind, and . . . put on the new man which was created according to God, in true righteousness and holiness . . . nor give place to the devil.

EPHESIANS 4:22–24, 27

Now therefore, listen to me, my children;
Pay attention to the words of my mouth:
Do not let your heart turn aside to her ways,
Do not stray into her paths;
For she has cast down many wounded,
And all who were slain by her were strong
    men.
Her house is the way to hell,
Descending to the chambers of death.

PROVERBS 7:24–27

The Lord knows how to deliver the godly out of temptations and to reserve the unjust under punishment for the day of judgment.

2 PETER 2:9

My brethren, count it all joy when you fall into various trials, knowing that the testing of your faith produces patience.

But let patience have its perfect work, that you may be perfect and complete, lacking nothing.

JAMES 1:2–4

Do not lust after her beauty in your heart,
Nor let her allure you with her eyelids.
For by means of a harlot
A man is reduced to a crust of bread;
And an adulteress will prey upon his precious life.

PROVERBS 6:25–26

Now therefore, listen to me, my children;
Pay attention to the words of my mouth:
Do not let your heart turn aside to her ways,
Do not stray into her paths;
For she has cast down many wounded,
And all who were slain by her were strong men.
Her house is the way to hell,
Descending to the chambers of death.

PROVERBS 7:24–27

Pride goes before destruction,
And a haughty spirit before a fall.
Better to be of a humble spirit with the lowly,
Than to divide the spoil with the proud.
He who heeds the word wisely will find good,
And whoever trusts in the LORD, happy is he.

PROVERBS 16:18–20

He who is of a proud heart stirs up strife,
But he who trusts in the LORD will be prospered.
He who trusts in his own heart is a fool,
But whoever walks wisely will be delivered.

PROVERBS 28:25–26

Then Jesus called a little child to Him, set him in the midst of them, and said, "Assuredly, I say to you, unless you are converted and become as little children, you will by no means enter the kingdom of heaven. Therefore whoever humbles himself as this little child is the greatest in the kingdom of heaven."

MATTHEW 18:2–4

But He gives more grace. Therefore He says: "God resists the proud, but gives grace to the humble."

Therefore submit to God. Resist the devil and he will flee from you.

Humble yourselves in the sight of the Lord, and He will lift you up.

JAMES 4:6–7, 10

Yet it shall not be so among you; but whoever desires to become great among you, let him be your servant

And whoever desires to be first among you, let him be your slave.

MATTHEW 20:26–27

Likewise you younger people, submit yourselves to your elders. Yes, all of you be submissive to one another, and be clothed with humility, for "God resists the proud, but gives grace to the humble."

Therefore humble yourselves under the mighty hand of God, that He may exalt you in due time.

1 PETER 5:5–6

But we have this treasure in earthen vessels, that the excellence of the power may be of God and not of us.

2 CORINTHIANS 4:7

Hear and give ear:
Do not be proud,
For the LORD has spoken.
Give glory to the LORD your God
Before He causes darkness,
And before your feet stumble
On the dark mountains,
And while you are looking for light,
He turns it into the shadow of death
And makes it dense darkness.
But if you will not hear it,
My soul will weep in secret for your pride;
My eyes will weep bitterly
And run down with tears,
Because the LORD's flock has been taken
       captive.

JEREMIAH 13:15-17

Take My yoke upon you and learn from Me, for I am gentle and lowly in heart, and you will find rest for your souls.

For My yoke is easy and My burden is light.

MATTHEW 11:29–30

The fear of the LORD is the instruction of wisdom, and before honor is humility.

PROVERBS 15:33

Death and life are in the power of the tongue, and those who love it will eat its fruit.

PROVERBS 18:21

Let no corrupt word proceed out of your mouth, but what is good for necessary edification, that it may impart grace to the hearers.

Let all bitterness, wrath, anger, clamor, and evil speaking be put away from you, with all malice.

And be kind to one another, tenderhearted, forgiving one another, just as God in Christ forgave you.

EPHESIANS 4:29, 31–32

Pleasant words are like a honeycomb, Sweetness to the soul and health to the bones.

PROVERBS 16:24

He who guards his mouth preserves his life, But he who opens wide his lips shall have destruction.

PROVERBS 13:3

A good man out of the good treasure of his heart brings forth good; and an evil man out of the evil treasure of his heart brings forth evil. For out of the abundance of the heart his mouth speaks.

LUKE 6:45

But I say to you that for every idle word men may speak, they will give account of it in the day of judgment.

MATTHEW 12:36

Sing to Him, sing psalms to Him; talk of all His wondrous works!

1 CHRONICLES 16:9

Whoever guards his mouth and tongue keeps his soul from troubles.

PROVERBS 21:23

Do not be a witness against your neighbor without cause, for would you deceive with your lips?

PROVERBS 24:28

Avoid foolish disputes, genealogies, contentions, and strivings about the law; for they are unprofitable and useless.

TITUS 3:9

O Timothy! Guard what was committed to your trust, avoiding the profane and idle babblings and contradictions of what is falsely called knowledge— by professing it some have strayed concerning the faith. Grace be with you. Amen.

1 TIMOTHY 6:20–21

> As long as my breath is in me,
> And the breath of God in my nostrils,
> My lips will not speak wickedness,
> Nor my tongue utter deceit.

JOB 27:3–4

As He who called you is holy, you also be holy in all your conduct.

1 PETER 1:15

Who, when He was reviled, did not revile in return; when He suffered, He did not threaten, but committed Himself to Him who judges righteously.

1 PETER 2:23

He who would love life and see good days, let him refrain his tongue from evil, and his lips from speaking deceit.

1 PETER 3:10

# How to Be Christ-Centered

Let the word of Christ dwell in you richly in all wisdom, teaching and admonishing one another in psalms and hymns and spiritual songs, singing with grace in your hearts to the Lord.

And whatever you do in word or deed, do all in the name of the Lord Jesus, giving thanks to God the Father through Him.

COLOSSIANS 3:16–17

I love those who love me, and those who seek me diligently will find me.

PROVERBS 8:17

Seek the LORD and His strength;
Seek His face evermore!
Remember His marvelous works which He
has done,
His wonders, and the judgments of His mouth,

1 CHRONICLES 16:11–12

Trust in Him at all times, you people; pour out your heart before Him; God is a refuge for us.

PSALM 62:8

You are My friends if you do whatever I command you.

No longer do I call you servants, for a servant does not know what his master is doing; but I have called you friends, for all things that I heard from My Father I have made known to you.

You did not choose Me, but I chose you and appointed you that you should go and bear fruit, and that your fruit should remain, that whatever you ask the Father in My name He may give you.

JOHN 15:14–16

Speaking to one another in psalms and hymns and spiritual songs, singing and making melody in your heart to the Lord, giving thanks always for all things to God the Father in the name of our Lord Jesus Christ.

EPHESIANS 5:19–20

I will bless the LORD at all times;
His praise shall continually be in my mouth.
My soul shall make its boast in the LORD;
The humble shall hear of it and be glad.
Oh, magnify the LORD with me,
And let us exalt His name together.
I sought the LORD, and He heard me,
And delivered me from all my fears.

PSALM 34:1–4

Truly my soul silently waits for God;
From Him comes my salvation.
He only is my rock and my salvation;
He is my defense;
I shall not be greatly moved.
My soul, wait silently for God alone,
For my expectation is from Him.
He only is my rock and my salvation;
He is my defense;
I shall not be moved.
In God is my salvation and my glory;
The rock of my strength,
And my refuge, is in God.

PSALM 62:1–2, 5–7

Put on the Lord Jesus Christ, and make no provision
for the flesh, to fulfill its lusts.

ROMANS 13:14

In You, O LORD, I put my trust;
Let me never be put to shame.
For You are my hope, O Lord GOD;
You are my trust from my youth.
Let my mouth be filled with Your praise
And with Your glory all the day.

PSALM 71:1, 5, 8

# Understanding the Liberty that Is in Christ

There is therefore now no condemnation to those who are in Christ Jesus, who do not walk according to the flesh, but according to the Spirit.

For the law of the Spirit of life in Christ Jesus has made me free from the law of sin and death.

ROMANS 8:1–2

For you, brethren, have been called to liberty; only do not use liberty as an opportunity for the flesh, but through love serve one another.

GALATIANS 5:13

There is neither Jew nor Greek, there is neither slave nor free, there is neither male nor female; for you are all one in Christ Jesus.

GALATIANS 3:28

But he who looks into the perfect law of liberty and continues in it, and is not a forgetful hearer but a doer of the work, this one will be blessed in what he does.

JAMES 1:25

Now the Lord is the Spirit; and where the Spirit of the Lord is, there is liberty.

2 CORINTHIANS 3:17

I, Jesus, have sent My angel to testify to you these things in the churches. I am the Root and the Offspring of David, the Bright and Morning Star.

And the Spirit and the bride say, "Come!" And let him who hears say, "Come!" And let him who thirsts come. Whoever desires, let him take the water of life freely.

REVELATION 22:16–17

"And you shall know the truth, and the truth shall make you free."

They answered Him, "We are Abraham's descendants, and have never been in bondage to anyone. How can you say, 'You will be made free'?"

Jesus answered them, "Most assuredly, I say to you, whoever commits sin is a slave of sin.

"And a slave does not abide in the house forever, but a son abides forever.

"Therefore if the Son makes you free, you shall be free indeed."

JOHN 8:32–36

Stand fast therefore in the liberty by which Christ has made us free, and do not be entangled again with a yoke of bondage.

GALATIANS 5:1

Am I not an apostle? Am I not free? Have I not seen Jesus Christ our Lord? Are you not my work in the Lord?

1 CORINTHIANS 9:1

And you shall know the truth, and the truth shall make you free.

Therefore if the Son makes you free, you shall be free indeed.

JOHN 8:32, 36

Now the Lord is the Spirit; and where the Spirit of the Lord is, there is liberty.

2 CORINTHIANS 3:17

Because the creation itself also will be delivered from the bondage of corruption into the glorious liberty of the children of God.

ROMANS 8:21

# HOW TO PRAISE THE LORD

Because Your lovingkindness is better than
    life,
My lips shall praise You.
Thus I will bless You while I live;
I will lift up my hands in Your name.
My soul shall be satisfied as with marrow and
    fatness,
And my mouth shall praise You with joyful
    lips.

PSALM 63:3–5

I will bless the LORD at all times; His praise shall continually be in my mouth.

PSALM 34:1

Accept, I pray, the freewill offerings of my mouth, O LORD, and teach me Your judgments.

PSALM 119:108

At midnight Paul and Silas were praying and singing hymns to God, and the prisoners were listening to them.

ACTS 16:25

Praise the LORD!
Sing to the LORD a new song,
And His praise in the assembly of saints.
Let Israel rejoice in their Maker;
Let the children of Zion be joyful in their
     King.
Let them praise His name with the dance;
Let them sing praises to Him with the timbrel
     and harp.
For the LORD takes pleasure in His people;
He will beautify the humble with salvation.
Let the saints be joyful in glory;
Let them sing aloud on their beds.
Let the high praises of God be in their mouth,
And a two-edged sword in their hand,

PSALM 149:1–6

Whoever offers praise glorifies Me; and to him who
orders his conduct aright I will show the salvation of
God.

PSALM 50:23

Praise the LORD!
Praise God in His sanctuary;
Praise Him in His mighty firmament!
Praise Him for His mighty acts;
Praise Him according to His excellent great-
      ness!
Praise Him with the sound of the trumpet;
Praise Him with the lute and harp!
Praise Him with the timbrel and dance;
Praise Him with stringed instruments and
      flutes!
Praise Him with loud cymbals;
Praise Him with clashing cymbals!
Let everything that has breath praise the
      LORD.
Praise the LORD!

PSALM 150:1–6


Praise the LORD!
Praise, O servants of the LORD,
Praise the name of the LORD!
Blessed be the name of the LORD
From this time forth and forevermore!
From the rising of the sun to its going down
The LORD's name is to be praised.

PSALM 113:1–3

"The voice of joy and the voice of gladness, the voice of the bridegroom and the voice of the bride, the voice of those who will say: 'Praise the LORD of hosts, for the LORD is good, for His mercy endures forever'—and of those who will bring the sacrifice of praise into the house of the LORD. For I will cause the captives of the land to return as at the first," says the LORD.

JEREMIAH 33:11

You are a chosen generation, a royal priesthood, a holy nation, His own special people, that you may proclaim the praises of Him who called you out of darkness into His marvelous light.

1 PETER 2:9

His lord said to him, "Well done, good and faithful servant; you were faithful over a few things, I will make you ruler over many things. Enter into the joy of your lord."

MATTHEW 25:21

These things I have spoken to you, that My joy may remain in you, and that your joy may be full.

This is My commandment, that you love one another as I have loved you.

JOHN 15:11–12

Let all those rejoice who put their trust in
    You;
Let them ever shout for joy, because You
    defend them;
Let those also who love Your name
Be joyful in You.
For You, O LORD, will bless the righteous;
With favor You will surround him as with a
    shield.

PSALM 5:11–12

263

A merry heart makes a cheerful countenance, but by sorrow of the heart the spirit is broken.

PROVERBS 15:13

God has not given us a spirit of fear, but of power and of love and of a sound mind.

2 TIMOTHY 1:7

The kingdom of God is not eating and drinking, but righteousness and peace and joy in the Holy Spirit.

For he who serves Christ in these things is acceptable to God and approved by men.

ROMANS 14:17–18

"Nevertheless do not rejoice in this, that the spirits are subject to you, but rather rejoice because your names are written in heaven."

In that hour Jesus rejoiced in the Spirit and said, "I thank You, Father, Lord of heaven and earth, that You have hidden these things from the wise and prudent and revealed them to babes. Even so, Father, for so it seemed good in Your sight."

LUKE 10:20–21

A merry heart does good, like medicine, but a broken spirit dries the bones.

PROVERBS 17:22

You love righteousness and hate wickedness;
Therefore God, Your God, has anointed You
With the oil of gladness more than Your com-
    panions.
All Your garments are scented with myrrh and
    aloes and cassia,
Out of the ivory palaces, by which they have
    made You glad.

PSALM 45:7–8

And you became followers of us and of the Lord, having received the word in much affliction, with joy of
the Holy Spirit.

1 THESSALONIANS 1:6

Restore to me the joy of Your salvation,
And uphold me by Your generous Spirit.
Then I will teach transgressors Your ways,
And sinners shall be converted to You.

PSALM 51:12–13

This is the day the LORD has made;
    we will rejoice and be glad in it.

PSALM 118:24

# MATURING IN CHRIST

Beloved, do not think it strange concerning the fiery
trial which is to try you, as though some strange thing
happened to you; but rejoice to the extent that you
partake of Christ's sufferings, that when His glory is
revealed, you may also be glad with exceeding joy.

Yet if anyone suffers as a Christian, let him not
be ashamed, but let him glorify God in this matter.

1 PETER 4:12–13, 16

> When you pass through the waters, I will be
>      with you;
> And through the rivers, they shall not over-
>      flow you.
> When you walk through the fire, you shall
>      not be burned,
> Nor shall the flame scorch you.
> For I am the LORD your God,
> The Holy One of Israel, your Savior;
> I gave Egypt for your ransom,
> Ethiopia and Seba in your place.

ISAIAH 43:2–3

But He knows the way that I take;
When He has tested me, I shall come forth as
      gold.
My foot has held fast to His steps;
I have kept His way and not turned aside.

JOB 23:10–11

The righteous cry out, and the LORD hears,
And delivers them out of all their troubles.
The LORD is near to those who have a broken
      heart,
And saves such as have a contrite spirit.
Many are the afflictions of the righteous,
But the LORD delivers him out of them all.

PSALM 34:17–19

For You will light my lamp;
The LORD my God will enlighten my darkness.
For by You I can run against a troop,
By my God I can leap over a wall.
As for God, His way is perfect;
The word of the LORD is proven;
He is a shield to all who trust in Him.
It is God who arms me with strength,
And makes my way perfect.

PSALM 18:28–30, 32

*God's Answers*

Blessed is the man who endures temptation; for when he has been approved, he will receive the crown of life which the Lord has promised to those who love Him.

JAMES 1:12

Though He slay me, yet will I trust Him.
Even so, I will defend my own ways before Him.
He also shall be my salvation,
For a hypocrite could not come before Him.

JOB 13:15–16

Deliver me out of the mire,
And let me not sink;
Let me be delivered from those who hate me,
And out of the deep waters.
Let not the floodwater overflow me,
Nor let the deep swallow me up;
And let not the pit shut its mouth on me.
Hear me, O LORD, for Your lovingkindness is
      good;
Turn to me according to the multitude of
      Your tender mercies.
And do not hide Your face from Your servant,
For I am in trouble;
Hear me speedily.
Draw near to my soul, and redeem it;
Deliver me because of my enemies.

PSALM 69:14–18

Is anyone among you sick? Let him call for the elders of the church, and let them pray over him, anointing him with oil in the name of the Lord.

And the prayer of faith will save the sick, and the Lord will raise him up. And if he has committed sins, he will be forgiven.

JAMES 5:14–15

You will keep him in perfect peace,
Whose mind is stayed on You,
Because he trusts in You.
Trust in the LORD forever,
For in YAH, the LORD, is everlasting strength.

ISAIAH 26:3–4

Heal me, O LORD, and I shall be healed; save me, and I shall be saved, for You are my praise.

JEREMIAH 17:14

Who Himself bore our sins in His own body on the tree, that we, having died to sins, might live for righteousness—by whose stripes you were healed.

1 PETER 2:24

And I said, "This is my anguish;
But I will remember the years of the right
    hand of the Most High."
I will remember the works of the LORD;
Surely I will remember Your wonders of old.
I will also meditate on all Your work,
And talk of Your deeds.
Your way, O God, is in the sanctuary;
Who is so great a God as our God?
You are the God who does wonders;
You have declared Your strength among the
    peoples.

PSALM 77:10-14

Yea, though I walk through the valley of the shadow
of death, I will fear no evil; for You are with me; Your
rod and Your staff, they comfort me.

PSALM 23:4

For we know that if our earthly house, this tent, is
destroyed, we have a building from God, a house not
made with hands, eternal in the heavens.

2 CORINTHIANS 5:1

For this is God, our God forever and ever; He will be
our guide even to death.

PSALM 48:14

But God will redeem my soul from the power of the grave, for He shall receive me.

PSALM 49:15


For all things are for your sakes, that grace, having spread through the many, may cause thanksgiving to abound to the glory of God.

Therefore we do not lose heart. Even though our outward man is perishing, yet the inward man is being renewed day by day.

For our light affliction, which is but for a moment, is working for us a far more exceeding and eternal weight of glory, while we do not look at the things which are seen, but at the things which are not seen. For the things which are seen are temporary, but the things which are not seen are eternal.

2 CORINTHIANS 4:15–18


I call to remembrance my song in the night; I meditate within my heart, and my spirit makes diligent search.

PSALM 77:6

Therefore, since Christ suffered for us in the flesh, arm yourselves also with the same mind, for he who has suffered in the flesh has ceased from sin, that he no longer should live the rest of his time in the flesh for the lusts of men, but for the will of God.

Beloved, do not think it strange concerning the fiery trial which is to try you, as though some strange thing happened to you; but rejoice to the extent that you partake of Christ's sufferings, that when His glory is revealed, you may also be glad with exceeding joy.

If you are reproached for the name of Christ, blessed are you, for the Spirit of glory and of God rests upon you. On their part He is blasphemed, but on your part He is glorified.

But let none of you suffer as a murderer, a thief, an evildoer, or as a busybody in other people's matters.

Yet if anyone suffers as a Christian, let him not be ashamed, but let him glorify God in this matter.

For the time has come for judgment to begin at the house of God; and if it begins with us first, what will be the end of those who do not obey the gospel of God?

1 PETER 4:1–2, 12–17

You therefore must endure hardship as a good soldier of Jesus Christ.

2 TIMOTHY 2:3

For whom the LORD loves He chastens, and scourges every son whom He receives.

If you endure chastening, God deals with you as with sons; for what son is there whom a father does not chasten?

But if you are without chastening, of which all have become partakers, then you are illegitimate and not sons.

Now no chastening seems to be joyful for the present, but painful; nevertheless, afterward it yields the peaceable fruit of righteousness to those who have been trained by it.

Therefore strengthen the hands which hang down, and the feeble knees, and make straight paths for your feet, so that what is lame may not be dislocated, but rather be healed.

HEBREWS 12:6–8,11–13

Blessed is the man who endures temptation; for when he has been approved, he will receive the crown of life which the Lord has promised to those who love Him.

JAMES 1:12

For what credit is it if, when you are beaten for your faults, you take it patiently? But when you do good and suffer, if you take it patiently, this is commendable before God.

For to this you were called, because Christ also suffered for us, leaving us an example, that you should follow His steps.

1 PETER 2:20–21

We see Jesus, who was made a little lower than the angels, for the suffering of death crowned with glory and honor, that He, by the grace of God, might taste death for everyone.

For it was fitting for Him, for whom are all things and by whom are all things, in bringing many sons to glory, to make the captain of their salvation perfect through sufferings.

HEBREWS 2:9–10

Though He was a Son, yet He learned obedience by the things which He suffered.

And having been perfected, He became the author of eternal salvation to all who obey Him.

HEBREWS 5:8–9

If children, then heirs—heirs of God and joint heirs with Christ, if indeed we suffer with Him, that we may also be glorified together.

For I consider that the sufferings of this present time are not worthy to be compared with the glory which shall be revealed in us.

ROMANS 8:17–18

The love of money is a root of all kinds of evil, for which some have strayed from the faith in their greediness, and pierced themselves through with many sorrows.

But you, O man of God, flee these things and pursue righteousness, godliness, faith, love, patience, gentleness.

1 TIMOTHY 6:10–11

Not that I speak in regard to need, for I have learned in whatever state I am, to be content: I know how to be abased, and I know how to abound. Everywhere and in all things I have learned both to be full and to be hungry, both to abound and to suffer need.

I can do all things through Christ who strengthens me.

PHILIPPIANS 4:11–13

Trust in the LORD, and do good;
Dwell in the land, and feed on His faithfulness.
Delight yourself also in the LORD,
And He shall give you the desires of your heart.

PSALM 37:3–4

Command those who are rich in this present age not to be haughty, nor to trust in uncertain riches but in the living God, who gives us richly all things to enjoy.

Let them do good, that they be rich in good works, ready to give, willing to share, storing up for themselves a good foundation for the time to come, that they may lay hold on eternal life.

1 TIMOTHY 6:17–19

Then He said to His disciples, "Therefore I say to you, do not worry about your life, what you will eat; nor about the body, what you will put on.

"Life is more than food, and the body is more than clothing.

"Consider the ravens, for they neither sow nor reap, which have neither storehouse nor barn; and God feeds them. Of how much more value are you than the birds?"

LUKE 12:22–24

So we may boldly say: "The LORD is my helper; I will not fear. What can man do to me?"

HEBREWS 13:6

My God shall supply all your need according to His riches in glory by Christ Jesus.

PHILIPPIANS 4:19

He who trusts in his riches will fall, but the righteous will flourish like foliage.

PROVERBS 11:28

There is one who makes himself rich, yet has nothing; and one who makes himself poor, yet has great riches.

Wealth gained by dishonesty will be diminished, but he who gathers by labor will increase.

PROVERBS 13:7, 11

Remove falsehood and lies far from me; give me neither poverty nor riches—feed me with the food allotted to me.

PROVERBS 30:8

For you have need of endurance, so that after you have done the will of God, you may receive the promise:

HEBREWS 10:36

Listen, my beloved brethren: Has God not chosen the poor of this world to be rich in faith and heirs of the kingdom which He promised to those who love Him?

JAMES 2:5

Peace I leave with you, My peace I give to you; not as the world gives do I give to you. Let not your heart be troubled, neither let it be afraid.

JOHN 14:27

Be anxious for nothing, but in everything by prayer and supplication, with thanksgiving, let your requests be made known to God; and the peace of God, which surpasses all understanding, will guard your hearts and minds through Christ Jesus.

Finally, brethren, whatever things are true, whatever things are noble, whatever things are just, whatever things are pure, whatever things are lovely, whatever things are of good report, if there is any virtue and if there is anything praiseworthy—meditate on these things.

PHILIPPIANS 4:6–8

Fear not, for I am with you;
Be not dismayed, for I am your God.
I will strengthen you,
Yes, I will help you,
I will uphold you with My righteous right hand.'

ISAIAH 41:10

He makes me to lie down in green pastures;
He leads me beside the still waters.
He restores my soul;
He leads me in the paths of righteousness
For His name's sake.
Yea, though I walk through the valley of the
      shadow of death,
I will fear no evil;
For You are with me;
Your rod and Your staff, they comfort me.

PSALM 23:2–4

Casting all your care upon Him, for He cares for you.

Be sober, be vigilant; because your adversary the devil walks about like a roaring lion, seeking whom he may devour.

Resist him, steadfast in the faith, knowing that the same sufferings are experienced by your brotherhood in the world.

But may the God of all grace, who called us to His eternal glory by Christ Jesus, after you have suffered a while, perfect, establish, strengthen, and settle you.

1 PETER 5:7–10

God is our refuge and strength,
A very present help in trouble.
Therefore we will not fear,
Even though the earth be removed,
And though the mountains be carried into the
    midst of the sea;
Though its waters roar and be troubled,
Though the mountains shake with its
    swelling. Selah

PSALM 46:1–3

"Be angry, and do not sin": do not let the sun go down on your wrath, nor give place to the devil.

EPHESIANS 4:26–27

But He was in the stern, asleep on a pillow. And they awoke Him and said to Him, "Teacher, do You not care that we are perishing?"

Then He arose and rebuked the wind, and said to the sea, "Peace, be still!" And the wind ceased and there was a great calm.

But He said to them, "Why are you so fearful? How is it that you have no faith?"

MARK 4:38–40

Surely He shall deliver you from the snare of
    the fowler
And from the perilous pestilence.
He shall cover you with His feathers,
And under His wings you shall take refuge;
His truth shall be your shield and buckler.
You shall not be afraid of the terror by night,
Nor of the arrow that flies by day,
Nor of the pestilence that walks in darkness,
Nor of the destruction that lays waste at
    noonday.
A thousand may fall at your side,
And ten thousand at your right hand;
But it shall not come near you.

PSALM 91:3–7

Whenever I am afraid,
I will trust in You.
In God (I will praise His word),
In God I have put my trust;
I will not fear.
What can flesh do to me?

PSALM 56:3–4

We are hard pressed on every side, yet not crushed; we are perplexed, but not in despair; persecuted, but not forsaken; struck down, but not destroyed—

Therefore we do not lose heart. Even though our outward man is perishing, yet the inward man is being renewed day by day.

For our light affliction, which is but for a moment, is working for us a far more exceeding and eternal weight of glory, while we do not look at the things which are seen, but at the things which are not seen. For the things which are seen are temporary, but the things which are not seen are eternal.

2 Corinthians 4:8–9, 16–18

Let your conduct be without covetousness; be content with such things as you have. For He Himself has said, "I will never leave you nor forsake you." So we may boldly say: "The Lord is my helper; I will not fear. What can man do to me?"

Hebrews 13:5–6

Come to Me, all you who labor and are heavy laden, and I will give you rest.

Matthew 11:28

For His anger is but for a moment,
His favor is for life;
Weeping may endure for a night,
But joy comes in the morning.
I cried out to You, O LORD;
And to the LORD I made supplication:
"What profit is there in my blood,
When I go down to the pit?
Will the dust praise You?
Will it declare Your truth?
Hear, O LORD, and have mercy on me;
LORD, be my helper!"
You have turned for me my mourning into
    dancing;
You have put off my sackcloth and clothed me
    with gladness,
To the end that my glory may sing praise to
    You and not be silent.
O LORD my God, I will give thanks to You
    forever.

PSALM 30:5, 8–12

This hope we have as an anchor of the soul, both sure and steadfast, and which enters the Presence behind the veil.

HEBREWS 6:19

Finally, brethren, whatever things are true, whatever things are noble, whatever things are just, whatever things are pure, whatever things are lovely, whatever things are of good report, if there is any virtue and if there is anything praiseworthy—meditate on these things.

PHILIPPIANS 4:8

> He has not dealt with us according to our
> sins,
> Nor punished us according to our iniquities.
> For as the heavens are high above the earth,
> So great is His mercy toward those who fear
> Him;
> As far as the east is from the west,
> So far has He removed our transgressions
> from us.

PSALM 103:10–12

After he had patiently endured, he obtained the promise.

HEBREWS 6:15

Let us not grow weary while doing good, for in due season we shall reap if we do not lose heart.

GALATIANS 6:9

Through the LORD's mercies we are not con-
　　sumed,
Because His compassions fail not.
They are new every morning;
Great is Your faithfulness.
"The LORD is my portion," says my soul,
"Therefore I hope in Him!"

LAMENTATIONS 3:22–24

But let us who are of the day be sober, putting on the
breastplate of faith and love, and as a helmet the hope
of salvation.

　　For God did not appoint us to wrath, but to
obtain salvation through our Lord Jesus Christ.

1 THESSALONIANS 5:8–9

Therefore do not worry about tomorrow, for tomorrow will worry about its own things. Sufficient for the
day is its own trouble.

MATTHEW 6:34

You are my hiding place and my shield; I hope in
Your word.

PSALM 119:114

Behold, the eye of the LORD is on those who
    fear Him,
On those who hope in His mercy,
To deliver their soul from death,
And to keep them alive in famine.
Our soul waits for the LORD;
He is our help and our shield.
For our heart shall rejoice in Him,
Because we have trusted in His holy name.
Let Your mercy, O LORD, be upon us,
Just as we hope in You.

PSALM 33:18–22

Let your conduct be without covetousness; be content with such things as you have. For He Himself has said, "I will never leave you nor forsake you."

So we may boldly say: "The LORD is my helper; I will not fear. What can man do to me?"

HEBREWS 13:5–6

Now may the God of hope fill you with all joy and peace in believing, that you may abound in hope by the power of the Holy Spirit.

ROMANS 15:13

Cast your burden on the LORD, and He shall sustain you; He shall never permit the righteous to be moved.

PSALM 55:22

> My soul, wait silently for God alone,
> For my expectation is from Him.
> He only is my rock and my salvation;
> He is my defense;
> I shall not be moved.
> In God is my salvation and my glory;
> The rock of my strength,
> And my refuge, is in God.

PSALM 62:5–7

> Those who wait on the LORD
> Shall renew their strength;
> They shall mount up with wings like eagles,
> They shall run and not be weary,
> They shall walk and not faint.

ISAIAH 40:31

Commit your way to the LORD,
Trust also in Him,
And He shall bring it to pass.
He shall bring forth your righteousness as the
      light,
And your justice as the noonday.
Rest in the LORD, and wait patiently for Him;
Do not fret because of him who prospers in
      his way,
Because of the man who brings wicked
      schemes to pass.

PSALM 37:5–7

There remains therefore a rest for the people of God.

Let us therefore be diligent to enter that rest, lest anyone fall according to the same example of disobedience.

Seeing then that we have a great High Priest who has passed through the heavens, Jesus the Son of God, let us hold fast our confession.

HEBREWS 4:9, 11, 14

He said, "My Presence will go with you, and I will give you rest."

EXODUS 33:14

Therefore, having been justified by faith, we have peace with God through our Lord Jesus Christ, through whom also we have access by faith into this grace in which we stand, and rejoice in hope of the glory of God.

ROMANS 5:1–2

We know that all things work together for good to those who love God, to those who are the called according to His purpose.

ROMANS 8:28

God is not the author of confusion but of peace, as in all the churches of the saints.

1 CORINTHIANS 14:33

Cast your burden on the LORD, and He shall sustain you; He shall never permit the righteous to be moved.

PSALM 55:22

The fear of man brings a snare, but whoever trusts in the LORD shall be safe.

PROVERBS 29:25

Blessed is the man who trusts in the LORD,
And whose hope is the LORD.
For he shall be like a tree planted by the waters,
Which spreads out its roots by the river,
And will not fear when heat comes;
But its leaf will be green,
And will not be anxious in the year of drought,
Nor will cease from yielding fruit.

JEREMIAH 17:7–8

We know that all things work together for good to those who love God, to those who are the called according to His purpose.

ROMANS 8:28

He will not be afraid of evil tidings;
His heart is steadfast, trusting in the LORD.
His heart is established;
He will not be afraid,
Until he sees his desire upon his enemies.

PSALM 112:7–8

I will say of the Lord, "He is my refuge and
    my fortress;
My God, in Him I will trust."
Surely He shall deliver you from the snare of
    the fowler
And from the perilous pestilence.
He shall cover you with His feathers,
And under His wings you shall take refuge;
His truth shall be your shield and buckler.

PSALM 91:2–4

Casting all your care upon Him, for He cares for you.
1 PETER 5:7

Yes, we had the sentence of death in ourselves, that
we should not trust in ourselves but in God who
raises the dead, who delivered us from so great a
death, and does deliver us; in whom we trust that He
will still deliver us.

2 CORINTHIANS 1:9–10

Therefore we will not fear, even though the earth be
removed, and though the mountains be carried into
the midst of the sea.

PSALM 46:2

*God's Answers*

Through God we will do valiantly, for it is He
    who shall tread down our enemies.

PSALM 60:12

The LORD is on my side;
I will not fear.
What can man do to me?
It is better to trust in the LORD
Than to put confidence in man.

PSALM 118:6, 8

He will not allow your foot to be moved; He
    who keeps you will not slumber.

PSALM 121:3

Those who trust in the LORD
Are like Mount Zion,
Which cannot be moved, but abides forever.
Do good, O LORD, to those who are good,
And to those who are upright in their hearts.

PSALM 125:1, 4

He who heeds the word wisely will find good, and
whoever trusts in the LORD, happy is he.

PROVERBS 16:20

The righteous shall flourish like a palm tree,
He shall grow like a cedar in Lebanon.
Those who are planted in the house of the
      LORD
Shall flourish in the courts of our God.
They shall still bear fruit in old age;
They shall be fresh and flourishing,
To declare that the LORD is upright;
He is my rock, and there is no
      unrighteousness in Him.

PSALM 92:12–15

For by me your days will be multiplied, and years of life will be added to you.

PROVERBS 9:11

Who satisfies your mouth with good things, so that your youth is renewed like the eagle's.

PSALM 103:5

Therefore remove sorrow from your heart, and put away evil from your flesh, for childhood and youth are vanity.

ECCLESIASTES 11:10

The days of our lives are seventy years;
And if by reason of strength they are eighty
      years,
Yet their boast is only labor and sorrow;
For it is soon cut off, and we fly away.
So teach us to number our days,
That we may gain a heart of wisdom.
Oh, satisfy us early with Your mercy,
That we may rejoice and be glad all our days!

PSALM 90:10, 12, 14

None of us lives to himself, and no one dies to himself.
    For if we live, we live to the Lord; and if we die, we die to the Lord. Therefore, whether we live or die, we are the Lord's.

ROMANS 14:7–8

For I know that my Redeemer lives,
And He shall stand at last on the earth;
And after my skin is destroyed, this I know,
That in my flesh I shall see God,
Whom I shall see for myself,
And my eyes shall behold, and not another.
How my heart yearns within me!

JOB 19:25–27

That the older men be sober, reverent, temperate, sound in faith, in love, in patience; the older women likewise, that they be reverent in behavior, not slanderers, not given to much wine, teachers of good things—that they admonish the young women to love their husbands, to love their children.

TITUS 2:2–4

For this is God, our God forever and ever;
He will be our guide even to death.

PSALM 48:14

The fear of the LORD prolongs days, but the years of the wicked will be shortened.

PROVERBS 10:27

You shall come to the grave at a full age, as a sheaf of grain ripens in its season.

JOB 5:26

For we know that if our earthly house, this tent, is destroyed, we have a building from God, a house not made with hands, eternal in the heavens.

2 CORINTHIANS 5:1

We do not look at the things which are seen, but at the things which are not seen. For the things which are seen are temporary, but the things which are not seen are eternal.

2 CORINTHIANS 4:18

When you pass through the waters, I will be
with you;
And through the rivers, they shall not overflow you.
When you walk through the fire, you shall
not be burned,
Nor shall the flame scorch you.

ISAIAH 43:2

Let all those rejoice who put their trust in
You;
Let them ever shout for joy, because You
defend them;
Let those also who love Your name
Be joyful in You.
For You, O LORD, will bless the righteous;
With favor You will surround him as with a
shield.

PSALM 5:11–12

The angel of the LORD encamps all around those who
fear Him, and delivers them.

PSALM 34:7

*God's Answers*

He who dwells in the secret place of the Most
    High
Shall abide under the shadow of the Almighty.
I will say of the LORD, "He is my refuge and
    my fortress;
My God, in Him I will trust."
Surely He shall deliver you from the snare of
    the fowler
And from the perilous pestilence.
He shall cover you with His feathers,
And under His wings you shall take refuge;
His truth shall be your shield and buckler.
You shall not be afraid of the terror by night,
Nor of the arrow that flies by day,
Nor of the pestilence that walks in darkness,
Nor of the destruction that lays waste at
    noonday.
A thousand may fall at your side,
And ten thousand at your right hand;
But it shall not come near you.
Only with your eyes shall you look,
And see the reward of the wicked.
Because you have made the LORD, who is my
    refuge,
Even the Most High, your dwelling place,
No evil shall befall you,
Nor shall any plague come near your dwelling.

PSALM 91:1–10

The horse is prepared for the day of battle, but deliverance is of the LORD.

PROVERBS 21:31

The fear of man brings a snare, but whoever trusts in the LORD shall be safe.

PROVERBS 29:25

I will both lie down in peace, and sleep; for You alone, O LORD, make me dwell in safety.

PSALM 4:8

> Yea, though I walk through the valley of the
>     shadow of death,
> I will fear no evil;
> For You are with me;
> Your rod and Your staff, they comfort me.

PSALM 23:4

> So shall they fear
> The name of the LORD from the west,
> And His glory from the rising of the sun;
> When the enemy comes in like a flood,
> The Spirit of the LORD will lift up a standard
>     against him.

ISAIAH 59:19

# How to Find Contentment

"Therefore do not worry, saying, 'What shall we eat?' or 'What shall we drink?' or 'What shall we wear?'

"For after all these things the Gentiles seek. For your heavenly Father knows that you need all these things.

"But seek first the kingdom of God and His righteousness, and all these things shall be added to you.

"Therefore do not worry about tomorrow, for tomorrow will worry about its own things. Sufficient for the day is its own trouble."

MATTHEW 6:31–34

You will keep him in perfect peace,
Whose mind is stayed on You,
Because he trusts in You.
Trust in the LORD forever,
For in YAH, the LORD, is everlasting strength.

ISAIAH 26:3–4

Let your conduct be without covetousness; be content with such things as you have. For He Himself has said, "I will never leave you nor forsake you."

So we may boldly say: "The LORD is my helper; I will not fear. What can man do to me?"

HEBREWS 13:5–6

Be anxious for nothing, but in everything by prayer and supplication, with thanksgiving, let your requests be made known to God; and the peace of God, which surpasses all understanding, will guard your hearts and minds through Christ Jesus.

Not that I speak in regard to need, for I have learned in whatever state I am, to be content: I know how to be abased, and I know how to abound. Everywhere and in all things I have learned both to be full and to be hungry, both to abound and to suffer need.

I can do all things through Christ who strengthens me.

PHILIPPIANS 4:6, 7, 11–13

We know that all things work together for good to those who love God, to those who are the called according to His purpose.

ROMANS 8:28

Now godliness with contentment is great gain.

For we brought nothing into this world, and it is certain we can carry nothing out.

And having food and clothing, with these we shall be content.

1 TIMOTHY 6:6–8

He who dwells in the secret place of the Most
    High
Shall abide under the shadow of the Almighty.
I will say of the LORD, "He is my refuge and
    my fortress;
My God, in Him I will trust."

PSALM 91:1–2

But I discipline my body and bring it into subjection,
lest, when I have preached to others, I myself should
become disqualified.

1 CORINTHIANS 9:27

The LORD upholds all who fall,
And raises up all who are bowed down.
The eyes of all look expectantly to You,
And You give them their food in due season.
You open Your hand
And satisfy the desire of every living thing.

PSALM 145:14–16

To be carnally minded is death, but to be spiritually
minded is life and peace.

ROMANS 8:6

# MINISTERING IN
# CHRIST

# WHAT IS TRUE SERVICE?

When He had called the people to Himself, with His disciples also, He said to them, "Whoever desires to come after Me, let him deny himself, and take up his cross, and follow Me.

"For whoever desires to save his life will lose it, but whoever loses his life for My sake and the gospel's will save it.

"For what will it profit a man if he gains the whole world, and loses his own soul?

"Or what will a man give in exchange for his soul?"

MARK 8:34–37

Abide in Me, and I in you. As the branch cannot bear fruit of itself, unless it abides in the vine, neither can you, unless you abide in Me.

I am the vine, you are the branches. He who abides in Me, and I in him, bears much fruit; for without Me you can do nothing.

JOHN 15:4–5

By this all will know that you are My disciples, if you have love for one another.

JOHN 13:35

He who calls you is faithful, who also will do it.

1 THESSALONIANS 5:24

For we do not preach ourselves, but Christ Jesus the Lord, and ourselves your bondservants for Jesus' sake.

For it is the God who commanded light to shine out of darkness, who has shone in our hearts to give the light of the knowledge of the glory of God in the face of Jesus Christ.

But we have this treasure in earthen vessels, that the excellence of the power may be of God and not of us.

2 CORINTHIANS 4:5–7

And whatever you do, do it heartily, as to the Lord and not to men, knowing that from the Lord you will receive the reward of the inheritance; for you serve the Lord Christ.

But he who does wrong will be repaid for what he has done, and there is no partiality.

COLOSSIANS 3:23–25

So the people asked him, saying, "What shall we do then?"

He answered and said to them, "He who has two tunics, let him give to him who has none; and he who has food, let him do likewise."

LUKE 3:10–11

You did not choose Me, but I chose you and appointed you that you should go and bear fruit, and that your fruit should remain, that whatever you ask the Father in My name He may give you.

These things I command you, that you love one another.

JOHN 15:16–17

That you may become blameless and harmless, children of God without fault in the midst of a crooked and perverse generation, among whom you shine as lights in the world, holding fast the word of life, so that I may rejoice in the day of Christ that I have not run in vain or labored in vain.

PHILIPPIANS 2:15–16

Command those who are rich in this present age not to be haughty, nor to trust in uncertain riches but in the living God, who gives us richly all things to enjoy.

Let them do good, that they be rich in good works, ready to give, willing to share, storing up for themselves a good foundation for the time to come, that they may lay hold on eternal life.

1 TIMOTHY 6:17–19

Be anxious for nothing, but in everything by prayer and supplication, with thanksgiving, let your requests be made known to God; and the peace of God, which surpasses all understanding, will guard your hearts and minds through Christ Jesus.

PHILIPPIANS 4:6–7

Assuredly, I say to you, whatever you bind on earth will be bound in heaven, and whatever you loose on earth will be loosed in heaven.

Again I say to you that if two of you agree on earth concerning anything that they ask, it will be done for them by My Father in heaven.

MATTHEW 18:18–19

Let us therefore come boldly to the throne of grace, that we may obtain mercy and find grace to help in time of need.

HEBREWS 4:16

Without faith it is impossible to please Him, for he who comes to God must believe that He is, and that He is a rewarder of those who diligently seek Him.

HEBREWS 11:6

*God's Answers*

Confess your trespasses to one another, and pray for
one another, that you may be healed. The effective,
fervent prayer of a righteous man avails much.

Elijah was a man with a nature like ours, and
he prayed earnestly that it would not rain; and it did
not rain on the land for three years and six months.

And he prayed again, and the heaven gave rain,
and the earth produced its fruit.

JAMES 5:16–18

Now in the morning, having risen a long while before
daylight, He went out and departed to a solitary
place; and there He prayed.

MARK 1:35

Now it came to pass in those days that He went out
to the mountain to pray, and continued all night in
prayer to God.

LUKE 6:12

LORD, I cry out to You;
Make haste to me!
Give ear to my voice when I cry out to You.
Let my prayer be set before You as incense,
The lifting up of my hands as the evening
      sacrifice.

PSALM 141:1–2

312

So shall My word be that goes forth from My mouth; it shall not return to Me void, but it shall accomplish what I please, and it shall prosper in the thing for which I sent it.

ISAIAH 55:11

So I say to you, ask, and it will be given to you; seek, and you will find; knock, and it will be opened to you.

LUKE 11:9

Then He spoke a parable to them, that men always ought to pray and not lose heart.

LUKE 18:1

> For the eyes of the LORD are on the righteous,
> And His ears are open to their prayers;
> But the face of the LORD is against those who do evil.

1 PETER 3:12

Evening and morning and at noon I will pray, and cry aloud, and He shall hear my voice.

PSALM 55:17

When you pray, you shall not be like the hypocrites. For they love to pray standing in the synagogues and on the corners of the streets, that they may be seen by men. Assuredly, I say to you, they have their reward.

But you, when you pray, go into your room, and when you have shut your door, pray to your Father who is in the secret place; and your Father who sees in secret will reward you openly.

MATTHEW 6:5–6

You are the light of the world. A city that is set on a hill cannot be hidden.

Nor do they light a lamp and put it under a basket, but on a lampstand, and it gives light to all who are in the house.

Let your light so shine before men, that they may see your good works and glorify your Father in heaven.

MATTHEW 5:14–16

No one, when he has lit a lamp, puts it in a secret place or under a basket, but on a lampstand, that those who come in may see the light.

LUKE 11:33

Therefore settle it in your hearts not to meditate beforehand on what you will answer; for I will give you a mouth and wisdom which all your adversaries will not be able to contradict or resist.

LUKE 21:14-15

I will sing to the LORD as long as I live;
I will sing praise to my God while I have my
being.

PSALM 104:33

But that the world may know that I love the Father,
and as the Father gave Me commandment, so I do.
Arise, let us go from here.

JOHN 14:31

Praying always with all prayer and supplication in the
Spirit, being watchful to this end with all perseverance and supplication for all the saints—and for me,
that utterance may be given to me, that I may open
my mouth boldly to make known the mystery of the
gospel, for which I am an ambassador in chains; that
in it I may speak boldly, as I ought to speak.

EPHESIANS 6:18–20

Therefore do not be ashamed of the testimony of our
Lord, nor of me His prisoner, but share with me in
the sufferings for the gospel according to the power of
God, who has saved us and called us with a holy calling, not according to our works, but according to His
own purpose and grace which was given to us in
Christ Jesus before time began, but has now been
revealed by the appearing of our Savior Jesus Christ,
who has abolished death and brought life and immortality to light through the gospel.

2 TIMOTHY 1:8–10

Finally, all of you be of one mind, having compassion for one another; love as brothers, be tenderhearted, be courteous; not returning evil for evil or reviling for reviling, but on the contrary blessing, knowing that you were called to this, that you may inherit a blessing.

For "He who would love life and see good days, let him refrain his tongue from evil, and his lips from speaking deceit.

Let him turn away from evil and do good; let him seek peace and pursue it.

But sanctify the Lord God in your hearts, and always be ready to give a defense to

everyone who asks you a reason for the hope that is in you, with meekness and fear.

1 PETER 3:8–11, 15

Also I say to you, whoever confesses Me before men, him the Son of Man also will confess before the angels of God.

But he who denies Me before men will be denied before the angels of God.

LUKE 12:8–9

The fruit of the righteous is a tree of life,
And he who wins souls is wise.

PROVERBS 11:30

Blessed are you when men hate you,
And when they exclude you,
And revile you, and cast out your name as evil,
For the Son of Man's sake.
Rejoice in that day and leap for joy!
For indeed your reward is great in heaven,
For in like manner their fathers did to the
            prophets.

LUKE 6:22–23

If the world hates you, you know that it hated Me before it hated you.

If you were of the world, the world would love its own. Yet because you are not of the world, but I chose you out of the world, therefore the world hates you.

Remember the word that I said to you, "A servant is not greater than his master." If they persecuted Me, they will also persecute you. If they kept My word, they will keep yours also.

But all these things they will do to you for My name's sake, because they do not know Him who sent Me.

JOHN 15:18–21

But even if you should suffer for righteousness' sake, you are blessed. And do not be afraid of their threats, nor be troubled.

But sanctify the Lord God in your hearts, and always be ready to give a defense to everyone who asks you a reason for the hope that is in you, with meekness and fear; having a good conscience, that when they defame you as evildoers, those who revile your good conduct in Christ may be ashamed.

1 PETER 3:14–16

If you are reproached for the name of Christ, blessed are you, for the Spirit of glory and of God rests upon you. On their part He is blasphemed, but on your part He is glorified.

Yet if anyone suffers as a Christian, let him not be ashamed, but let him glorify God in this matter.

1 PETER 4:14, 16

Therefore, having been justified by faith, we have peace with God through our Lord Jesus Christ, through whom also we have access by faith into this grace in which we stand, and rejoice in hope of the glory of God.

ROMANS 5:1–2

*God's Answers*

The LORD has been my defense,
And my God the rock of my refuge.
He has brought on them their own iniquity,
And shall cut them off in their own wicked-
    ness;
The LORD our God shall cut them off.

PSALM 94:22–23

My eyes shall be on the faithful of the land,
That they may dwell with me;
He who walks in a perfect way,
He shall serve me.
He who works deceit shall not dwell within
    my house;
He who tells lies shall not continue in my
    presence.

PSALM 101:6–7

Persecutions, afflictions, which happened to me at Antioch, at Iconium, at Lystra—what persecutions I endured. And out of them all the Lord delivered me.

Yes, and all who desire to live godly in Christ Jesus will suffer persecution.

2 TIMOTHY 3:11–12

Do not say, "I will recompense evil"; wait for the LORD, and He will save you.

PROVERBS 20:22

320

# UNDERSTANDING THE
# LEADING OF THE LORD

The LORD will guide you continually,
And satisfy your soul in drought,
And strengthen your bones;
You shall be like a watered garden,
And like a spring of water, whose waters do
      not fail.

ISAIAH 58:11

I say to you that likewise there will be more joy in heaven over one sinner who repents than over ninety-nine just persons who need no repentance.

LUKE 15:7

"For My thoughts are not your thoughts,
Nor are your ways My ways," says the LORD.
"For as the heavens are higher than the earth,
So are My ways higher than your ways,
And My thoughts than your thoughts."

ISAIAH 55:8–9

Beloved, do not believe every spirit, but test the spirits, whether they are of God; because many false prophets have gone out into the world.

1 JOHN 4:1

The Lord is not slack concerning His promise, as some count slackness, but is longsuffering toward us, not willing that any should perish but that all should come to repentance.

2 PETER 3:9

The Son of Man has come to save that which was lost.

MATTHEW 18:11

The spirit of a man is the lamp of the LORD, searching all the inner depths of his heart.

PROVERBS 20:27

> He found him in a desert land
> And in the wasteland, a howling wilderness;
> He encircled him, He instructed him,
> He kept him as the apple of His eye.
> As an eagle stirs up its nest,
> Hovers over its young,
> Spreading out its wings, taking them up,
> Carrying them on its wings,
> So the LORD alone led him,
> And there was no foreign god with him.
>
> DEUTERONOMY 32:10–12

So he shepherded them according to the integrity of his heart, and guided them by the skillfulness of his hands.

Psalm 78:72

> You shall not go out with haste,
> Nor go by flight;
> For the Lord will go before you,
> And the God of Israel will be your rear guard.

Isaiah 52:12

There are three that bear witness in heaven: the Father, the Word, and the Holy Spirit; and these three are one.

1 John 5:7

> A man's heart plans his way,
> But the Lord directs his steps.
> The lot is cast into the lap,
> But its every decision is from the Lord.

Proverbs 16:9, 33

God has not given us a spirit of fear, but of power and of love and of a sound mind.

2 Timothy 1:7

Rest in the LORD, and wait patiently for Him;
Do not fret because of him who prospers in
      his way,
Because of the man who brings wicked
      schemes to pass.
Cease from anger, and forsake wrath;
Do not fret—it only causes harm.
For evildoers shall be cut off;
But those who wait on the LORD,
They shall inherit the earth.

PSALM 37:7–9

I waited patiently for the LORD;
And He inclined to me,
And heard my cry.
He also brought me up out of a horrible pit,
Out of the miry clay,
And set my feet upon a rock,
And established my steps.
He has put a new song in my mouth—
Praise to our God;
Many will see it and fear,
And will trust in the LORD.

PSALM 40:1–3

The LORD will wait, that He may be gracious to you; and therefore He will be exalted, that He may have mercy on you. For the LORD is a God of justice; blessed are all those who wait for Him.

ISAIAH 30:18

> Indeed, let no one who waits on You be
>     ashamed;
> Let those be ashamed who deal treacherously
>     without cause.
> Show me Your ways, O LORD;
> Teach me Your paths.
> Lead me in Your truth and teach me,
> For You are the God of my salvation;
> On You I wait all the day.
> Let integrity and uprightness preserve me,
> For I wait for You.

PSALM 25:3–5, 21

Wait on the LORD; be of good courage, and He shall strengthen your heart; wait, I say, on the LORD!

PSALM 27:14

I will look to the LORD; I will wait for the God of my salvation; my God will hear me.

MICAH 7:7

*God's Answers*

Those who wait on the LORD
Shall renew their strength;
They shall mount up with wings like eagles,
They shall run and not be weary,
They shall walk and not faint.

Isaiah 40:31

The LORD is good to those who wait for Him,
To the soul who seeks Him.
It is good that one should hope and wait quietly
For the salvation of the LORD.

Lamentations 3:25–26

My soul, wait silently for God alone,
For my expectation is from Him.
He only is my rock and my salvation;
He is my defense;
I shall not be moved.

Psalm 62:5–6

And it will be said in that day:
"Behold, this is our God;
We have waited for Him, and He will save us.
This is the LORD;
We have waited for Him;
We will be glad and rejoice in His salvation."

ISAIAH 25:9


Let us hold fast the confession of our hope without wavering, for He who promised is faithful.

HEBREWS 10:23

That all the peoples of the earth may know that the LORD is God; there is no other.

Let your heart therefore be loyal to the LORD our God, to walk in His statutes and keep His commandments, as at this day.

1 KINGS 8:60–61

Be doers of the word, and not hearers only, deceiving yourselves.

JAMES 1:22

Now therefore, if you will indeed obey My voice and keep My covenant, then you shall be a special treasure to Me above all people; for all the earth is Mine.

EXODUS 19:5

Do not be deceived, God is not mocked; for whatever a man sows, that he will also reap.

For he who sows to his flesh will of the flesh reap corruption, but he who sows to the Spirit will of the Spirit reap everlasting life.

GALATIANS 6:7–8

If you love Me, keep My commandments.

JOHN 14:15

But Peter and the other apostles answered and said: "We ought to obey God rather than men."

ACTS 5:29

I discipline my body and bring it into subjection, lest, when I have preached to others, I myself should become disqualified.

1 CORINTHIANS 9:27

Casting down arguments and every high thing that exalts itself against the knowledge of God, bringing every thought into captivity to the obedience of Christ.

2 CORINTHIANS 10:5

Whoever has no rule over his own spirit is like a city broken down, without walls.

PROVERBS 25:28

He who is faithful in what is least is faithful also in much; and he who is unjust in what is least is unjust also in much.

LUKE 16:10

Behold, You desire truth in the inward parts, and in the hidden part You will make me to know wisdom.

PSALM 51:6

*God's Answers*

The world is passing away, and the lust of it; but he who does the will of God abides forever.

1 JOHN 2:17

If anyone does not abide in Me, he is cast out as a branch and is withered; and they gather them and throw them into the fire, and they are burned.

If you abide in Me, and My words abide in you, you will ask what you desire, and it shall be done for you.

If you keep My commandments, you will abide in My love, just as I have kept My Father's commandments and abide in His love.

JOHN 15:6–7, 10

Now the just shall live by faith; but if anyone draws back, My soul has no pleasure in him.

HEBREWS 10:38

Then Samuel said:
Has the LORD as great delight in burnt offer-
   ings and sacrifices,
As in obeying the voice of the LORD?
Behold, to obey is better than sacrifice,
And to heed than the fat of rams.

1 SAMUEL 15:22

Do not lay up for yourselves treasures on earth, where moth and rust destroy and where thieves break in and steal; but lay up for yourselves treasures in heaven, where neither moth nor rust destroys and where thieves do not break in and steal.

For where your treasure is, there your heart will be also.

MATTHEW 6:19–21

Now Jesus sat opposite the treasury and saw how the people put money into the treasury. And many who were rich put in much.

Then one poor widow came and threw in two mites, which make a quadrans.

So He called His disciples to Himself and said to them, "Assuredly, I say to you that this poor widow has put in more than all those who have given to the treasury; for they all put in out of their abundance, but she out of her poverty put in all that she had, her whole livelihood."

MARK 12:41–44

Give to the LORD the glory due His name; bring an offering, and come into His courts.

PSALM 96:8

But this I say: He who sows sparingly will also reap sparingly, and he who sows bountifully will also reap bountifully.

So let each one give as he purposes in his heart, not grudgingly or of necessity; for God loves a cheerful giver.

2 CORINTHIANS 9:6–7

But woe to you Pharisees! For you tithe mint and rue and all manner of herbs, and pass by justice and the love of God. These you ought to have done, without leaving the others undone.

LUKE 11:42

He who is faithful in what is least is faithful also in much; and he who is unjust in what is least is unjust also in much.

Therefore if you have not been faithful in the unrighteous mammon, who will commit to your trust the true riches?

LUKE 16:10–11

He who has a generous eye will be blessed, for he gives of his bread to the poor.

PROVERBS 22:9

Therefore bear fruits worthy of repentance, and do not think to say to yourselves, "We have Abraham as our father." For I say to you that God is able to raise up children to Abraham from these stones.

MATTHEW 3:8–9

Does he thank that servant because he did the things that were commanded him? I think not.

So likewise you, when you have done all those things which you are commanded, say, "We are unprofitable servants. We have done what was our duty to do."

LUKE 17:9–10

As soon as the commandment was circulated, the children of Israel brought in abundance the firstfruits of grain and wine, oil and honey, and of all the produce of the field; and they brought in abundantly the tithe of everything.

2 CHRONICLES 31:5

# HOPING IN CHRIST

That if you confess with your mouth the Lord Jesus and believe in your heart that God has raised Him from the dead, you will be saved.

For with the heart one believes unto righteousness, and with the mouth confession is made unto salvation.

For the Scripture says, "Whoever believes on Him will not be put to shame."

For there is no distinction between Jew and Greek, for the same Lord over all is rich to all who call upon Him.

For "whoever calls on the name of the LORD shall be saved."

ROMANS 10:9–13

Seek the LORD while He may be found,
Call upon Him while He is near.
Let the wicked forsake his way,
And the unrighteous man his thoughts;
Let him return to the LORD,
And He will have mercy on him;
And to our God,
For He will abundantly pardon.

ISAIAH 55:6–7

Behold, I stand at the door and knock. If anyone
hears My voice and opens the door, I will come in to
him and dine with him, and he with Me.

REVELATION 3:20

All that the Father gives Me will come to Me, and the
one who comes to Me I will by no means cast out.

And this is the will of Him who sent Me, that
everyone who sees the Son and believes in Him may
have everlasting life; and I will raise him up at the
last day.

No one can come to Me unless the Father who
sent Me draws him; and I will raise him up at the last
day.

It is written in the prophets, "And they shall all
be taught by God." Therefore everyone who has
heard and learned from the Father comes to Me.

Not that anyone has seen the Father, except He
who is from God; He has seen the Father.

Most assuredly, I say to you, he who believes in
Me has everlasting life.

JOHN 6:37, 40, 44–47

Without faith it is impossible to please Him, for he
who comes to God must believe that He is, and that
He is a rewarder of those who diligently seek Him.

HEBREWS 11:6

The Lord is not slack concerning His promise, as some count slackness, but is longsuffering toward us, not willing that any should perish but that all should come to repentance.

But grow in the grace and knowledge of our Lord and Savior Jesus Christ. To Him be the glory both now and forever. Amen.

2 PETER 3:9, 18

Having been set free from sin, and having become slaves of God, you have your fruit to holiness, and the end, everlasting life.

For the wages of sin is death, but the gift of God is eternal life in Christ Jesus our Lord.

ROMANS 6:22–23

Come now, you who say, "Today or tomorrow we will go to such and such a city, spend a year there, buy and sell, and make a profit"; whereas you do not know what will happen tomorrow. For what is your life? It is even a vapor that appears for a little time and then vanishes away.

Instead you ought to say, "If the Lord wills, we shall live and do this or that."

JAMES 4:13–15

Draw near to God and He will draw near to you. Cleanse your hands, you sinners; and purify your hearts, you double-minded.

Lament and mourn and weep! Let your laughter be turned to mourning and your joy to gloom.

Humble yourselves in the sight of the Lord, and He will lift you up.

JAMES 4:8–10

I love those who love me, and those who seek me diligently will find me.

PROVERBS 8:17

Seek the LORD and His strength;
Seek His face evermore!
Remember His marvelous works which He
    has done,
His wonders, and the judgments of His
    mouth,

1 CHRONICLES 16:11–12

In the day when I cried out, You answered me, and made me bold with strength in my soul.

PSALM 138:3

Then you will call upon Me and go and pray to Me, and I will listen to you.

And you will seek Me and find Me, when you search for Me with all your heart.

JEREMIAH 29:12–13

As the deer pants for the water brooks,
So pants my soul for You, O God.
My soul thirsts for God, for the living God.
When shall I come and appear before God?
Deep calls unto deep at the noise of Your
    waterfalls;
All Your waves and billows have gone over me.
The LORD will command His lovingkindness
    in the daytime,
And in the night His song shall be with me—
A prayer to the God of my life.

PSALM 42:1–2, 7–8

In my distress I called upon the LORD, and cried out to my God; He heard my voice from His temple, and my cry came before Him, even to His ears.

PSALM 18:6

The LORD is near to all who call upon Him, to all who call upon Him in truth.

PSALM 145:18

Hear my cry, O God;
Attend to my prayer.
From the end of the earth I will cry to You,
When my heart is overwhelmed;
Lead me to the rock that is higher than I.

PSALM 61:1–2


My soul, wait silently for God alone, for my expectation is from Him.

PSALM 62:5


All that the Father gives Me will come to Me, and the one who comes to Me I will by no means cast out.

JOHN 6:37


And the Spirit and the bride say, "Come!" And let him who hears say, "Come!" And let him who thirsts come. Whoever desires, let him take the water of life freely.

REVELATION 22:17

# How to Recover Spiritually

Have you not known?
Have you not heard?
The everlasting God, the LORD,
The Creator of the ends of the earth,
Neither faints nor is weary.
His understanding is unsearchable.
He gives power to the weak,
And to those who have no might He increases
    strength.
But those who wait on the LORD
Shall renew their strength;
They shall mount up with wings like eagles,
They shall run and not be weary,
They shall walk and not faint.

                   ISAIAH 40:28–29, 31


For You, Lord, are good, and ready to forgive,
And abundant in mercy to all those who call
    upon You.
Give ear, O LORD, to my prayer;
And attend to the voice of my supplications.
In the day of my trouble I will call upon You,
For You will answer me.

                      PSALM 86:5–7

I will heal their backsliding, I will love them freely, for My anger has turned away from him.

HOSEA 14:4

"I will seek what was lost and bring back what was driven away, bind up the broken and strengthen what was sick; but I will destroy the fat and the strong, and feed them in judgment.

"Thus they shall know that I, the LORD their God, am with them, and they, the house of Israel, are My people," says the Lord GOD. "You are My flock, the flock of My pasture; you are men, and I am your God."

EZEKIEL 34:16, 30–31

He who covers his sins will not prosper, but whoever confesses and forsakes them will have mercy.

PROVERBS 28:13

> Before I was afflicted I went astray,
> But now I keep Your word.
> You are good, and do good;
> Teach me Your statutes.

PSALM 119:67–68

Poverty and shame will come to him who disdains correction, but he who regards a rebuke will be honored.

PROVERBS 13:18

Now no chastening seems to be joyful for the present, but painful; nevertheless, afterward it yields the peaceable fruit of righteousness to those who have been trained by it.

Therefore strengthen the hands which hang down, and the feeble knees, and make straight paths for your feet, so that what is lame may not be dislocated, but rather be healed.

Pursue peace with all people, and holiness, without which no one will see the Lord.

HEBREWS 12:11–14

Blessed is the man whom You instruct, O
    LORD,
And teach out of Your law,
That You may give him rest from the days of
    adversity,
Until the pit is dug for the wicked.
For the LORD will not cast off His people,
Nor will He forsake His inheritance.

PSALM 94:12–14

When my soul fainted within me,
I remembered the LORD;
And my prayer went up to You,
Into Your holy temple.

JONAH 2:7

By which have been given to us exceedingly great and precious promises, that through these you may be partakers of the divine nature, having escaped the corruption that is in the world through lust.

But also for this very reason, giving all diligence, add to your faith virtue, to virtue knowledge, to knowledge self-control, to self-control perseverance, to perseverance godliness, to godliness brotherly kindness, and to brotherly kindness love.

For if these things are yours and abound, you will be neither barren nor unfruitful in the knowledge of our Lord Jesus Christ.

2 PETER 1:4–8

Let us hold fast the confession of our hope without wavering, for He who promised is faithful.

Therefore do not cast away your confidence, which has great reward.

For you have need of endurance, so that after you have done the will of God, you may receive the promise: For yet a little while, and He who is coming will come and will not tarry.

HEBREWS 10:23, 35–37

If you carefully keep all these commandments which I command you to do—to love the LORD your God, to walk in all His ways, and to hold fast to Him—then the LORD will drive out all these nations from before you, and you will dispossess greater and mightier nations than yourselves.

DEUTERONOMY 11:22–23

Only be strong and very courageous, that you may observe to do according to all the law which Moses My servant commanded you; do not turn from it to the right hand or to the left, that you may prosper wherever you go.

JOSHUA 1:7

For assuredly, I say to you, whoever says to this mountain, "Be removed and be cast into the sea," and does not doubt in his heart, but believes that those things he says will be done, he will have whatever he says.

MARK 11:23

Do not become sluggish, but imitate those who through faith and patience inherit the promises.

HEBREWS 6:12

Now faith is the substance of things hoped for, the evidence of things not seen.

But without faith it is impossible to please Him, for he who comes to God must believe that He is, and that He is a rewarder of those who diligently seek Him.

By faith Sarah herself also received strength to conceive seed, and she bore a child when she was past the age, because she judged Him faithful who had promised.

HEBREWS 11:1, 6, 11

Now this is the confidence that we have in Him, that if we ask anything according to His will, He hears us.

And if we know that He hears us, whatever we ask, we know that we have the petitions that we have asked of Him.

1 JOHN 5:14–15

If you are willing and obedient,
You shall eat the good of the land;
But if you refuse and rebel,
You shall be devoured by the sword";
For the mouth of the LORD has spoken.

ISAIAH 1:19–20

If any of you lacks wisdom, let him ask of God, who gives to all liberally and without reproach, and it will be given to him.

But let him ask in faith, with no doubting, for he who doubts is like a wave of the sea driven and tossed by the wind.

For let not that man suppose that he will receive anything from the Lord; he is a double-minded man, unstable in all his ways.

JAMES 1:5–8

For with God nothing will be impossible.

LUKE 1:37

Behold, the LORD's hand is not shortened,
That it cannot save;
Nor His ear heavy,
That it cannot hear.
But your iniquities have separated you from
    your God;
And your sins have hidden His face from you,
So that He will not hear.

ISAIAH 59:1–2

But seek first the kingdom of God and His right-eousness, and all these things shall be added to you.

MATTHEW 6:33

# UNDERSTANDING IN CHRIST

As for God, His way is perfect;
The word of the LORD is proven;
He is a shield to all who trust in Him.
For who is God, except the LORD?
And who is a rock, except our God?
It is God who arms me with strength,
And makes my way perfect.

PSALM 18:30–32

"For My thoughts are not your thoughts,
Nor are your ways My ways," says the LORD.
"For as the heavens are higher than the earth,
So are My ways higher than your ways,
And My thoughts than your thoughts."

ISAIAH 55:8–9

Jesus said to them, "Have you never read in
        the Scriptures:
"The stone which the builders rejected
Has become the chief cornerstone.
This was the LORD's doing,
And it is marvelous in our eyes"?

MATTHEW 21:42

350

Though the LORD is on high,
Yet He regards the lowly;
But the proud He knows from afar.
Though I walk in the midst of trouble, You
    will revive me;
You will stretch out Your hand
Against the wrath of my enemies,
And Your right hand will save me.

                        PSALM 138:6–7


He has made the earth by His power,
He has established the world by His wisdom,
And has stretched out the heavens at His
    discretion.

                        JEREMIAH 10:12


The LORD is in His holy temple,
The LORD's throne is in heaven;
His eyes behold,
His eyelids test the sons of men.
The LORD tests the righteous,
But the wicked and the one who loves vio-
    lence His soul hates.
For the LORD is righteous,
He loves righteousness;
His countenance beholds the upright.

                        PSALM 11:4–5, 7

I, the LORD, search the heart,
I test the mind,
Even to give every man according to his ways,
According to the fruit of his doings.

JEREMIAH 17:10

Now therefore, let the fear of the LORD be upon you;
take care and do it, for there is no iniquity with the
LORD our God, no partiality, nor taking of bribes.

2 CHRONICLES 19:7

As a father pities his children,
So the LORD pities those who fear Him.
For He knows our frame;
He remembers that we are dust.

PSALM 103:13–14

If you then, being evil, know how to give good gifts to
your children, how much more will your Father who
is in heaven give good things to those who ask Him!

MATTHEW 7:11

Every good gift and every perfect gift is from above,
and comes down from the Father of lights, with
whom there is no variation or shadow of turning.

JAMES 1:17

The fear of the LORD is the beginning of wisdom; a good understanding have all those who do His commandments. His praise endures forever.

PSALM 111:10

Counsel is mine, and sound wisdom; I am understanding, I have strength.

PROVERBS 8:14

Forsake foolishness and live, and go in the way of understanding. "The fear of the LORD is the beginning of wisdom, and the knowledge of the Holy One is understanding.

PROVERBS 9:6, 10

How much better to get wisdom than gold! And to get understanding is to be chosen rather than silver. The highway of the upright is to depart from evil; he who keeps his way preserves his soul.

PROVERBS 16:16–17

Understanding is a wellspring of life to him who has it. But the correction of fools is folly.

PROVERBS 16:22

Yes, if you cry out for discernment,
And lift up your voice for understanding,
If you seek her as silver,
And search for her as for hidden treasures;
Then you will understand the fear of the
    LORD,
And find the knowledge of God.
For the LORD gives wisdom;
From His mouth come knowledge and under-
    standing;
He stores up sound wisdom for the upright;
He is a shield to those who walk uprightly;
He guards the paths of justice,
And preserves the way of His saints.
Then you will understand righteousness and
    justice,
Equity and every good path.
When wisdom enters your heart,
And knowledge is pleasant to your soul,
Discretion will preserve you;
Understanding will keep you,

PROVERBS 2:3–11

If any of you lacks wisdom, let him ask of God, who gives to all liberally and without reproach, and it will be given to him.

JAMES 1:5

Incline your ear, and come to Me.
Hear, and your soul shall live;
And I will make an everlasting covenant
   with you—
The sure mercies of David.
Seek the LORD while He may be found,
Call upon Him while He is near.
"For My thoughts are not your thoughts,
Nor are your ways My ways," says the LORD.
"For as the heavens are higher than the earth,
So are My ways higher than your ways,
And My thoughts than your thoughts.

ISAIAH 55:3, 6, 8–9

But there is a spirit in man, and the breath of the Almighty gives him understanding.

JOB 32:8

The LORD is righteous in all His ways,
Gracious in all His works.
The LORD is near to all who call upon Him,
To all who call upon Him in truth.
He will fulfill the desire of those who fear Him;
He also will hear their cry and save them.

PSALM 145:17–19

He does not delight in the strength of the horse;
He takes no pleasure in the legs of a man.
The LORD takes pleasure in those who fear
      Him,
In those who hope in His mercy.

PSALM 147:10–11

If you seek her as silver,
And search for her as for hidden treasures;
Then you will understand the fear of the LORD,
And find the knowledge of God.

PROVERBS 2:4–5

The fear of the LORD is the beginning of wisdom, and
the knowledge of the Holy One is understanding.

PROVERBS 9:10

The fear of the LORD is the instruction of wisdom, and before honor is humility.

PROVERBS 15:33

The fear of the LORD is the beginning of knowledge, but fools despise wisdom and instruction.

PROVERBS 1:7

> In the fear of the LORD there is strong
> confidence,
> And His children will have a place of refuge.
> The fear of the LORD is a fountain of life,
> To turn one away from the snares of death.

PROVERBS 14:26-27

The fear of the LORD leads to life, and he who has it will abide in satisfaction; he will not be visited with evil.

PROVERBS 19:23

And to man He said, "Behold, the fear of the Lord, that is wisdom, and to depart from evil is understanding."

JOB 28:28

The fear of the LORD prolongs days, but the years of the wicked will be shortened.

PROVERBS 10:27

*God's Answers*

Oh, fear the LORD, you His saints! There is no want to those who fear Him.

PSALM 34:9

Praise the LORD! Blessed is the man who fears the LORD, who delights greatly in His commandments.

PSALM 112:1

> Let us hear the conclusion of the whole matter:
> Fear God and keep His commandments,
> For this is man's all.
> For God will bring every work into judgment,
> Including every secret thing,
> Whether good or evil.

ECCLESIASTES 12:13–14

All nations before Him are as nothing,
And they are counted by Him less than
    nothing and worthless.
To whom then will you liken God?
Or what likeness will you compare to Him?
"To whom then will you liken Me,
Or to whom shall I be equal?" says the Holy
    One.
Lift up your eyes on high,
And see who has created these things,
Who brings out their host by number;
He calls them all by name,
By the greatness of His might
And the strength of His power;
Not one is missing.
Have you not known?
Have you not heard?
The everlasting God, the LORD,
The Creator of the ends of the earth,
Neither faints nor is weary.
His understanding is unsearchable.

ISAIAH 40:17, 18, 25, 26, 28

Great is the LORD, and greatly to be praised;
And His greatness is unsearchable.
One generation shall praise Your works to
    another,
And shall declare Your mighty acts.
Your kingdom is an everlasting kingdom,
And Your dominion endures throughout all
    generations.

PSALM 145:3–4, 13

The LORD is our Judge, the LORD is our Lawgiver, the LORD is our King; He will save us.

ISAIAH 33:22

Behold, I am the LORD, the God of all flesh. Is there anything too hard for Me?

JEREMIAH 32:27

The heavens declare the glory of God; and the firmament shows His handiwork.

PSALM 19:1

Whom have I in heaven but You? And there is none upon earth that I desire besides You.

PSALM 73:25

Thus says the LORD:
"Heaven is My throne,
And earth is My footstool.
Where is the house that you will build Me?
And where is the place of My rest?
For all those things My hand has made,
And all those things exist,"
Says the LORD.
"But on this one will I look:
On him who is poor and of a contrite spirit,
And who trembles at My word."

ISAIAH 66:1–2

"Am I a God near at hand," says the LORD,
"And not a God afar off?
Can anyone hide himself in secret places,
So I shall not see him?" says the LORD;
"Do I not fill heaven and earth?" says the LORD.

JEREMIAH 23:23–24

"Where were you when I laid the foundations of the earth?

Tell Me, if you have understanding.
Who determined its measurements?
Surely you know!
Or who stretched the line upon it?
To what were its foundations fastened?
Or who laid its cornerstone,
When the morning stars sang together,
And all the sons of God shouted for joy?

JOB 38:4–7

And I heard a loud voice from heaven saying, "Behold, the tabernacle of God is with men, and He will dwell with them, and they shall be His people. God Himself will be with them and be their God.

"And God will wipe away every tear from their eyes; there shall be no more death, nor sorrow, nor crying. There shall be no more pain, for the former things have passed away."

Then He who sat on the throne said, "Behold, I make all things new." And He said to me, "Write, for these words are true and faithful."

And He said to me, "It is done! I am the Alpha and the Omega, the Beginning and the End. I will give of the fountain of the water of life freely to him who thirsts.

REVELATION 21:3–6

And when I saw Him, I fell at His feet as dead. But He laid His right hand on me, saying to me, "Do not be afraid; I am the First and the Last.

"I am He who lives, and was dead, and behold, I am alive forevermore. Amen. And I have the keys of Hades and of Death."

REVELATION 1:17–18

Assuredly, I say to you, I will no longer drink of the fruit of the vine until that day when I drink it new in the kingdom of God.

MARK 14:25

But as it is written: "Eye has not seen, nor ear heard, nor have entered into the heart of man the things which God has prepared for those who love Him."

But God has revealed them to us through His Spirit. For the Spirit searches all things, yes, the deep things of God.

For what man knows the things of a man except the spirit of the man which is in him? Even so no one knows the things of God except the Spirit of God.

1 CORINTHIANS 2:9–11

Those who are wise shall shine
Like the brightness of the firmament,
And those who turn many to righteousness
Like the stars forever and ever.

DANIEL 12:3

Surely goodness and mercy shall follow me all the days of my life; and I will dwell in the house of the LORD forever.

PSALM 23:6

*God's Answers*

Violence shall no longer be heard in your land,
Neither wasting nor destruction within your
      borders;
But you shall call your walls Salvation,
And your gates Praise.
The sun shall no longer be your light by day,
Nor for brightness shall the moon give light
      to you;
But the LORD will be to you an everlasting
      light,
And your God your glory.
Your sun shall no longer go down,
Nor shall your moon withdraw itself;
For the LORD will be your everlasting light,
And the days of your mourning shall be ended.

ISAIAH 60:18–20


For since the beginning of the world
Men have not heard nor perceived by the ear,
Nor has the eye seen any God besides You,
Who acts for the one who waits for Him.

ISAIAH 64:4


For now we see in a mirror, dimly, but then face to
face. Now I know in part, but then I shall know just
as I also am known.

1 CORINTHIANS 13:12

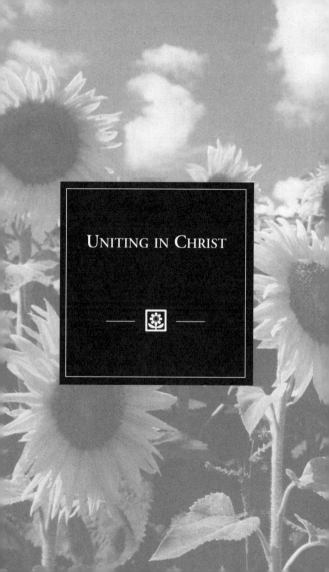

# UNITING IN CHRIST

For you are still carnal. For where there are envy, strife, and divisions among you, are you not carnal and behaving like mere men?

For when one says, "I am of Paul," and another, "I am of Apollos," are you not carnal?

Who then is Paul, and who is Apollos, but ministers through whom you believed, as the Lord gave to each one?

I planted, Apollos watered, but God gave the increase.

So then neither he who plants is anything, nor he who waters, but God who gives the increase.

Now he who plants and he who waters are one, and each one will receive his own reward according to his own labor.

For we are God's fellow workers; you are God's field, you are God's building.

1 CORINTHIANS 3:3–9

But now God has set the members, each one of them, in the body just as He pleased.

And if they were all one member, where would the body be?

But now indeed there are many members, yet one body.

And the eye cannot say to the hand, "I have no need of you"; nor again the head to the feet, "I have no need of you."

No, much rather, those members of the body which seem to be weaker are necessary.

And those members of the body which we think to be less honorable, on these we bestow greater honor; and our unpresentable parts have greater modesty, but our presentable parts have no need. But God composed the body, having given greater honor to that part which lacks it, that there should be no schism in the body, but that the members should have the same care for one another.

And if one member suffers, all the members suffer with it; or if one member is honored, all the members rejoice with it.

Now you are the body of Christ, and members individually.

1 CORINTHIANS 12:18–27

Now, therefore, you are no longer strangers and for-
eigners, but fellow citizens with the saints and members of the household of God, having been built on
the foundation of the apostles and prophets, Jesus
Christ Himself being the chief cornerstone, in whom
the whole building, being joined together, grows into
a holy temple in the Lord, in whom you also are
being built together for a dwelling place of God in
the Spirit.

EPHESIANS 2:19–22

Finally, all of you be of one mind, having compassion
for one another; love as brothers, be tenderhearted, be
courteous; not returning evil for evil or reviling for
reviling, but on the contrary blessing, knowing that
you were called to this, that you may inherit a blessing.

1 PETER 3:8–9

For where two or three are gathered together in My name, I am there in the midst of them."

Then Peter came to Him and said, "Lord, how often shall my brother sin against me, and I forgive him? Up to seven times?"

Jesus said to him, "I do not say to you, up to seven times, but up to seventy times seven.

MATTHEW 18:20–22

You call me Teacher and Lord, and you say well, for so I am.

If I then, your Lord and Teacher, have washed your feet, you also ought to wash one another's feet.

For I have given you an example, that you should do as I have done to you.

Most assuredly, I say to you, a servant is not greater than his master; nor is he who is sent greater than he who sent him.

If you know these things, blessed are you if you do them.

JOHN 13:13–17

The Lord is not slack concerning His promise, as some count slackness, but is longsuffering toward us, not willing that any should perish but that all should come to repentance.

2 PETER 3:9

> Arise, shine;
> For your light has come!
> And the glory of the LORD is risen upon you.
> For behold, the darkness shall cover the earth,
> And deep darkness the people;
> But the LORD will arise over you,
> And His glory will be seen upon you.

ISAIAH 60:1–2

Therefore be patient, brethren, until the coming of the Lord. See how the farmer waits for the precious fruit of the earth, waiting patiently for it until it receives the early and latter rain.

JAMES 5:7

The earth will be filled with the knowledge of the glory of the LORD, as the waters cover the sea.

HABAKKUK 2:14

And they shall rebuild the old ruins,
They shall raise up the former desolations,
And they shall repair the ruined cities,
The desolations of many generations.
For as the earth brings forth its bud,
As the garden causes the things that are sown
     in it to spring forth,
So the Lord GOD will cause righteousness and
     praise to spring forth before all the
     nations.

ISAIAH 61:4, 11


All the ends of the world
Shall remember and turn to the LORD,
And all the families of the nations
Shall worship before You.
For the kingdom is the LORD's,
And He rules over the nations.

PSALM 22:27–28


This gospel of the kingdom will be preached in all the
world as a witness to all the nations, and then the end
will come.

MATTHEW 24:14

And it shall come to pass afterward
That I will pour out My Spirit on all flesh;
Your sons and your daughters shall prophesy,
Your old men shall dream dreams,
Your young men shall see visions.
And also on My menservants and on My
     maidservants
I will pour out My Spirit in those days.
And I will show wonders in the heavens and
     in the earth:
Blood and fire and pillars of smoke.
The sun shall be turned into darkness,
And the moon into blood,
Before the coming of the great and awesome
     day of the LORD.
And it shall come to pass
That whoever calls on the name of the LORD
Shall be saved.
For in Mount Zion and in Jerusalem there
     shall be deliverance,
As the LORD has said,
Among the remnant whom the LORD calls.

JOEL 2:28–32

Behold, I will do a new thing, now it shall spring forth; shall you not know it? I will even make a road in the wilderness and rivers in the desert.

ISAIAH 43:19

But know this, that in the last days perilous times will come: For men will be lovers of themselves, lovers of money, boasters, proud, blasphemers, disobedient to parents, unthankful, unholy, unloving, unforgiving, slanderers, without self-control, brutal, despisers of good, traitors, headstrong, haughty, lovers of pleasure rather than lovers of God, having a form of godliness but denying its power. And from such people turn away!

2 TIMOTHY 3:1–5

Christ was offered once to bear the sins of many. To those who eagerly wait for Him He will appear a second time, apart from sin, for salvation.

HEBREWS 9:28

And in the latter time of their kingdom, when the transgressors have reached their fullness, a king shall arise, having fierce features, who understands sinister schemes.

DANIEL 8:23

And Jesus answered and said to them: "Take heed that no one deceives you.

"For many will come in My name, saying, 'I am the Christ,' and will deceive many.

"And you will hear of wars and rumors of wars. See that you are not troubled; for all these things must come to pass, but the end is not yet.

"For nation will rise against nation, and kingdom against kingdom. And there will be famines, pestilences, and earthquakes in various places.

"All these are the beginning of sorrows.

"Then they will deliver you up to tribulation and kill you, and you will be hated by all nations for My name's sake.

"And then many will be offended, will betray one another, and will hate one another.

"Then many false prophets will rise up and deceive many.

"And because lawlessness will abound, the love of many will grow cold.

"But he who endures to the end shall be saved.

"And this gospel of the kingdom will be preached in all the world as a witness to all the nations, and then the end will come.

MATTHEW 24:4–14

Then two men will be in the field: one will be taken and the other left.

Watch therefore, for you do not know what hour your Lord is coming.

Therefore you also be ready, for the Son of Man is coming at an hour you do not expect.

MATTHEW 24:40, 42, 44

Now the Spirit expressly says that in latter times some will depart from the faith, giving heed to deceiving spirits and doctrines of demons, speaking lies in hypocrisy, having their own conscience seared with a hot iron, forbidding to marry, and commanding to abstain from foods which God created to be received with thanksgiving by those who believe and know the truth.

1 TIMOTHY 4:1–3

But you, beloved, remember the words which were spoken before by the apostles of our Lord Jesus Christ: how they told you that there would be mockers in the last time who would walk according to their own ungodly lusts.

These are sensual persons, who cause divisions, not having the Spirit.

But you, beloved, building yourselves up on your most holy faith, praying in the Holy Spirit, keep yourselves in the love of God, looking for the mercy of our Lord Jesus Christ unto eternal life.

JUDE 17–21

## • NOTES •

• PRAYER JOURNAL •

• NOTES •

• PRAYER JOURNAL •

_____

_____

_____

_____

_____

_____

_____

_____

_____

_____

_____

_____

_____

_____

_____

_____

_____

_____

_____

_____

_____

• PRAYER JOURNAL •

_____
_____
_____
_____
_____
_____
_____
_____
_____
_____
_____
_____
_____
_____
_____
_____
_____
_____
_____
_____
_____
_____

• PRAYER JOURNAL •

## • PRAYER JOURNAL •